EQUALITY FOR I

MW00479385

This book offers a new and compelling account of distributive justice and its relation to choice. Unlike luck egalitarians, who treat unchosen differences in people's circumstances as sources of unjust inequality to be overcome, Sher views such differences as pervasive and unavoidable features of the human situation. Appealing to an original account of what makes us moral equals, he argues that our interest in successfully negotiating life's ever-shifting contingencies is more basic than our interest in achieving any more specific goals. He argues, also, that the state's obligation to promote this interest supports a principled version of the view that what matters about resources, opportunity, and other secondary goods is only that each person have enough. The book opens up a variety of new questions, and offers a distinctive new perspective for scholars of political theory and political philosophy, and for those interested in distributive justice and luck egalitarianism.

GEORGE SHER is Herbert S. Autrey Professor of Philosophy at Rice University. His publications include *Desert* (1987), *Beyond Neutrality: Perfectionism and Politics* (Cambridge, 1997), and *Who Knew? Responsibility without Awareness* (2009).

EQUALITY FOR INEGALITARIANS

GEORGE SHER

CAMBRIDGE
UNIVERSITY PRESS

CAMBRIDGE
UNIVERSITY PRESS

University Printing House, Cambridge CB2 8BS, United Kingdom

Cambridge University Press is part of the University of Cambridge.

It furthers the University's mission by disseminating knowledge in the pursuit of
education, learning and research at the highest international levels of excellence.

www.cambridge.org
Information on this title: www.cambridge.org/9780521251709

First published 2014

Printed in the United Kingdom by Clays, St Ives plc

A catalogue record for this publication is available from the British Library

Library of Congress Cataloguing in Publication data
Sher, George.
Equality for Inegalitarians / George Sher.
pages cm
Includes bibliographical references and index.
ISBN 978-1-107-00957-8 (hardback) – ISBN 978-0-521-25170-9 (pbk.)
1. Distributive justice. 2. Equality. I. Title.
HB523.S5325 2014
340′.115 – dc23 2014021795

ISBN 978-1-107-00957-8 Hardback
ISBN 978-0-521-25170-9 Paperback

Contents

Preface

In Houston, where I live, my favorite supermarket is located near a halfway house. Its residents dot the neighborhood, and one has a regular place outside the market. He's a damaged person, confined to a wheelchair, and he spends a lot of time staring at the ground. Sometimes, though, I see him in conversation with the security guard. He's not too damaged to have a life.

What kind of life? It's a mystery to me, and I wonder about it often. There must be things he likes, little treats, and he must have some kind of social world complete with intrigues, slights, and a complicated pecking order. But life in a wheelchair looks hard, certainly because of restriction and dependency, perhaps also because of discomfort and/or shame. Are his consolations restricted to drink and drugs? Does he read? *Can* he read? What does the future look like to him?

His is, I'm sure, not an easy life. But is it also an unjust life – one that, in a more just society, would be different and better? Has his government failed him by allowing him to live as he does?

Philosophers have proposed many theories that address this question, and with this book I join their ranks. When I began, the book's aim and scope were relatively modest. I have long been attracted to the ideal of equal opportunity, and like many others, I had come to regard the view known as luck egalitarianism – very roughly, that inequalities are just if and only if they are due to the parties' choices rather than luck – as an attractive elaboration of that ideal. However, at the same time, it seemed to me that luck egalitarianism raised deep analytical and normative problems that had not been recognized, much less resolved, by its proponents. Thus, at the outset, my aim was simply to bring to light, and if possible to resolve, the most important of these neglected problems. By doing this, I hoped to produce an improved and defensible version of luck egalitarianism.

But that's not what happened; for the more I thought about why a person's choices should affect what he ought to have, the more I became convinced that we cannot make sense of this without abandoning several key elements of luck egalitarianism. More specifically, I came to believe that we cannot account for the normative significance of choice – the luck egalitarian's fundamental insight – without assigning new and radically different roles to both equality and luck.

Here is the short version of the view at which I arrived. I now believe that the reason people should be allowed to enjoy or suffer the consequences of their choices is not that they are responsible for those outcomes (although they often are), but rather that no one can genuinely live a life of his own unless his decisions have a real impact on his fortunes. I believe, as well, that given our unique relation to our own lives, the non-comparative facts about a person's life are morally more important than whether he fares better or worse than others. For this reason, I take the distributive implications of the moral equality of persons to be considerably more complex than is generally supposed. And, finally, given what is involved in living a characteristically human life, I view the innumerable contingencies that differentiate each person's situation from those of others not as so many sources of unjust inequality to be neutralized by society, but rather as the backdrop in whose absence we could not live recognizably human lives at all.

Because this is a work of philosophy, my defense of these claims, and of the larger account of distributive justice of which they are elements, is pitched at a rather high level of abstraction. However, because the problem the account is intended to solve is very much a human one, it is natural to want to bring the discussion back to earth. What does an outlook like mine imply about the abundant misery and gross disparities of wealth by which we are surrounded? What, in particular, do they imply about the man in the wheelchair?

To this last question, the quick answer is that I cannot know because I don't know *him*. However, even allowing for this, some things can be said. No less than any luck egalitarian, I believe it would be relevant to know whether the man's poverty and disability are the result of certain headstrong or careless choices he made when he was younger, or whether, instead, he was born with a congenital condition that left him unemployable, or awoke one morning to find that the economy simply had no place for him. However, unlike many luck egalitarians, I don't think this question is decisive in either direction. On the one hand, because lives are lived over time, whatever case there is for allowing the consequences of the man's earlier choices to play themselves out must be tempered by the need to preserve his ability to shape the later parts of his life. On the other, even if his economic options were from the beginning more limited than those of others, their impact on his overall ability to shape his life remains a further question. Because our lives are bounded by ever-changing sets of contingent circumstances — because different people are born in different areas, exposed to different influences, meet different others, acquire different information, and so on without end — no single element of a person's circumstances can be decisive in determining what sorts of lives are open to him. Thus, while it may well be true that our man is owed far more than our social arrangements have managed to deliver, the injustice, if it exists, is no simple function of the disadvantages that so readily elicit our sympathy, concern, and guilt.

In the course of writing this book, I have accumulated a variety of intellectual debts, and it is a pleasure to acknowledge these here. Those who commented helpfully on different parts of the book, or who made useful suggestions in discussions of its topics, include Richard Arneson, Baruch Brody, Anthony Carreras, Mark Fleurbeay, Moti Gorin, Stan Husi, Simon Keller, Steven Macedo, Kristi Olson, Allen Patton, Lisa Rasmussen, Adina Roskies, Larry Temkin, Andrew Williams, and Hector Wittwer. I also received useful comments from the members of a number of audiences, from a thoughtful clearance reviewer for Cambridge University Press, and from the members of a particularly productive seminar at Rice University who discussed much of this material in draft form: Dan Burkett, Chris Dohna, Beth Hupfer, Sherry Kao, Carissa Phillips-Garrett, Victor Saenz, Graham Valenta, Brandon Williams, and Peter Zuk. I had the privilege of spending the 2011–12 academic year in the stimulating environment of the Princeton University Center for Human Values, and I gratefully acknowledge both the support that I received there and the research leave from Rice that made my visit possible. Some of the material in Chapter 3 originally appeared in *Social Philosophy and Policy*, 27, 1 (Winter 2010) under the title "Real-World Luck Egalitarianism."

As always, my greatest debt is to my wife Emily Fox Gordon. In addition to providing her usual invaluable stylistic advice, she was tireless in reassuring me that the world needs not only another book on equality, but this book in particular. I still don't know if that's true, but there's no one I trust more, so maybe it is.

CHAPTER I

Reconciling equality and choice

My aim in this book is to take a fresh look at two widely accepted ideas, and in so doing to shed new light on some old questions of distributive justice.

The ideas I have in mind — that all persons have equal claims to whatever benefits their society provides and that each person's choices should play a central role in shaping his own life — have both been accommodated, in one way or another, by every theory of justice of which I know. However, the theory that has addressed them most explicitly is the one that has become known as luck egalitarianism. In its simplest form, luck egalitarianism asserts that inequalities are just if and only if they are not due to luck. Put a bit more precisely and decomposed into conjuncts, it asserts, first, that all inequalities that cannot be traced to the parties' own choices are unjust, and so should be evened out, but, second, that any inequalities that *are* due to differences in the parties' choices are indeed just (or at least consistent with justice) as long as the options among which the parties chose were themselves sufficiently equal.[1]

---

[1] The literature on luck egalitarianism is voluminous, but any short list of important texts would include Gerald Cohen, "On the Currency of Egalitarian Justice," *Ethics* 99 (July 1989): 906–47; Richard Arneson, "Equality and Equal Opportunity for Welfare," *Philosophical Studies* 56 (1989): 77–93; Richard Arneson, "Luck Egalitarianism: An Interpretation and Defense," *Philosophical Topics* 32 (2004): 1–20; John Roemer, *Equality of Opportunity* (Cambridge, MA: Harvard University Press, 1998); and Eric Rakowski, *Equal Justice* (Oxford University Press, 1991). For two more recent book-length treatments, see Susan Hurley, *Justice, Luck, and Knowledge* (Cambridge, MA: Harvard University Press, 2003) and Carl Knight, *Luck Egalitarianism* (University of Edinburgh Press, 2009). For important critical discussion, see Elizabeth Anderson, "What Is the Point of Equality?" *Ethics* 109 (1999): 287–337,

I think, in fact, that luck egalitarianism is untenable for a variety of reasons, and that any theory that successfully integrates the claims of choice and equality will have to abandon its conjunctive approach in favor of some different structure. However, although luck egalitarianism has had plenty of critics, the difficulties that I view as most serious have received surprisingly little attention. For this reason, I will devote the first half of this book to a critical discussion that brings those difficulties into the open. Then, guided by what has emerged, I will propose and defend an integrated account of a very different sort.

I

Although Ronald Dworkin rejects the label "luck egalitarian," that view has its origins in his magisterial "What Is Equality" essays, first published in 1981.[2] At a somewhat greater remove, the view obviously draws inspiration from Rawls's influential claims, advanced in *A Theory of Justice* in 1971, that the distribution of talents and abilities among persons is "decided by the outcome of a natural lottery" which is "arbitrary from a moral perspective,"[3] and hence that "[t]here is no more reason to permit the distribution of income and wealth to be settled by the distribution of natural assets than by historical and social fortune."[4] Since the publication of Dworkin's groundbreaking essays, there has been a steady outpouring of work, written by some of the best political philosophers of our time, refining and elaborating his attempt to reconcile justice with choice. This work has addressed such questions as exactly where to make the cut between just and unjust

---

and Samuiel Scheffler, "What Is Egalitarianism?" *Philosophy and Public Affairs* 31 (2003): 5–39.

[2] Ronald Dworkin, "What Is Equality? Part 1: Equality of Welfare," *Philosophy and Public Affairs* 10 1981): 185–246, and Ronald Dworkin, "What Is Equality? Part 2: Equality of Resources," 10 (1981): 283–345. Both essays are reprinted as chapters in Ronald Dworkin, *Sovereign Virtue* (Cambridge, MA: Harvard University Press, 2000).

[3] John Rawls, *A Theory of Justice* (Cambridge, MA: Harvard University Press, 1971), p. 74.

[4] *Ibid.*

inequalities,[5] how we can best operationalize the idea of the proportion of a person's income that is due to his own efforts,[6] and whether what should replace an unchosen inequality is a fully equal distribution or only the movement toward equality that results from assigning priority to the well-being of the less well off or providing a satisfactory minimum for everyone.[7] In addition, philosophers working within the rubric of luck egalitarianism have continued to advance the debate about which goods are most directly relevant to distributive justice.[8]

But while luck egalitarians have indeed devoted much energy and attention to working out the details of their position and rebutting objections to it, they have devoted far less to the rationale for either its egalitarian or its inegalitarian conjunct. It is more or less common ground among them that inequalities that are due to luck are unjust; that any inequality that is unchosen is *ipso facto* a matter of luck; and that justice therefore requires the mitigation if not the elimination of all such inequalities. I believe, and will argue at length in what

[5] In "On the Currency of Distributive Justice," Cohen influentially criticizes Dworkin's claim that the crucial distinction is the one that divides actions that originate in the agent himself from those whose sources are external, while others have questioned the relevance of Dworkin's brute luck/option luck distinction. On the latter issue, see Kasper Lippert-Rasmussen, "Egalitarianism, Option Luck, and Responsibility," *Ethics* 111 (2001): 548–79; Peter Vallentyne, "Brute Luck Option Luck, and Equality of Initial Opportunities," *Ethics* 112 (2002): 529–57; and Martin Sandbu, "On Dworkin's Brute-Luck – Option-Luck Distinction and the Consistency of Brute-Luck Egalitarianism," *Politics, Philosophy and Economics* 3 (2004): 283–312.

[6] John Roemer explores this question in a number of works including *Equality of Opportunity* and "Equality and Responsibility," *The Boston Review* 20 (1995): 3–7.

[7] From his early essay "On the Currency of Distributive Justice" through his last major work *Rescuing Justice and Equality* (Cambridge, MA: Harvard University Press, 2008), Gerald Cohen was a consistent champion of straight equality. For defense of equality against a prioritarian challenge, see Larry Temkin, "Egalitarianism Defended," *Ethics* 113 (2003): 764–82. By contrast, Arneson now favors a view which he calls "responsibility-catering prioritarianism": see Richard Arneson, "Luck Egalitarianism and Prioritarianism," *Ethics* 110 (2000): 339–49.

[8] In addition to the familiar alternatives of welfare, resources, and opportunities, a number of hybrid candidates have emerged. Thus, in "On the Currency of Egalitarian Justice," Cohen straddles the line between welfare and resources by urging the equalization of a hybrid good, "advantage," which combines the two; while in "Equality and Equal Opportunity for Welfare," Arneson argues that what should be equalized are opportunities to satisfy preferences.

follows, that what Susan Hurley calls "the luck-neutralizing aim" rests on a fundamental misunderstanding of the roles of both choice and contingency in human affairs. However, for now, it is sufficient to note that even if we grant that aim, we will still have a lot of ground to cover before we are entitled to accept either conjunct of luck egalitarianism.

For, as Hurley has correctly pointed out, it simply does not follow, from the premise that an unchosen inequality is unjust, that it is any more just to (re)distribute the relevant goods equally among the affected parties. It would take some further argument to establish equality (or any other distributive pattern) as the default position. In addition – a separate point – the premise that unchosen inequalities are unjust also does not imply that all (or even any) of the inequalities that *do* reflect the parties' choices therefore *are* just. There is nothing inconsistent about maintaining both that all unchosen inequalities are unjust and that all inequalities that can be traced to the parties' choices are unjust as well.

Thus, even if we agree that all unchosen inequalities are unjust, we will still need two further arguments, one to justify the luck egalitarian's egalitarian conjunct and another to justify his inegalitarian conjunct. Moreover, at least offhand, these justifications seem likely to be in tension with each other, since the stronger the case for distributive equality becomes, the harder it becomes to defend deviations from it. This raises the important (though rarely asked) question of how the justifications of the two conjuncts might be related.

There are two basic possibilities, in that the justifications might be either independent or linked. On the one hand, they will be independent if the case for the egalitarian conjunct rests on some general principle of equality while the case for the inegalitarian conjunct rests on some further choice-related principle or value – for example, one which demands that each person get what he deserves or what he is responsible for bringing about. By contrast, the two justifications will be linked if it is the case either that one is somehow implicit in the other or that they can both be traced to the same deeper principle or value. In what follows, I will refer to justifications of the first sort as pluralistic and the second as monistic.

Because the normative foundations of luck egalitarianism are so underdiscussed, it is often hard to discern which justificatory approach its proponents have in mind. However, given the paucity of attempts to produce a unified justification, it seems safe to assume that most luck egalitarians are pluralists. This, I think, is to be expected; for our moral vocabulary contains a rich array of choice-related notions — control, responsibility, and desert are three of the most prominent — which have no obvious connections with equality. These notions are ready to hand, and many find them compelling. Also, of course, to ground the inegalitarian conjunct of luck egalitarianism in an apparently free-standing moral notion is not to rule out the possibility of unearthing a deeper connection between that notion and equality at some later point.

II

Is there a convincing pluralistic justification of luck egalitarianism? I think, in fact, that the answer is "no," but I will not be able to explain why until I have confronted the main pluralistic options in Chapters 2 and 3. Thus, for now, I will offer only a few general reasons for skepticism.

The most obvious problem with the pluralistic approach is its lack of specificity. By this I mean not merely that the pluralistic luck egalitarian needs to specify which of the relevant choice-related notions he takes to ground his inegalitarian conjunct, but also, and more importantly, that he owes us an explanation of when, and why, the normative demands of choice dominate those of equality and when and why they are dominated by them. This last point is important because any luck egalitarian who lacks a principled account of the conditions under which choice-related considerations take precedence over equality will also be incapable of drawing a principled line between those inequalities that are and are not just. Because pluralism is theoretically unambitious, and provides no overarching account of the relative strength of the principles or values it identifies as relevant, its proponents will have difficulty responding both to those critics who view equality as so important that it always takes precedence over all competing values and to those others who are willing to accept any amount of social or economic inequality as long as it can somehow be traced to the parties' earlier choices. By contrast, if luck egalitarians can manage a monistic defense of their position, then they may indeed be able to answer both sets of critics; for if the demands of equality and inequality are unified at some deeper level, then it may be possible to adjudicate between the claims of equality and choice by extracting an account of the proper boundaries of each from their common source.

For these and other reasons, I regard the monistic approach as more promising than its pluralistic rival. However, I also believe that it is precisely by taking the monistic approach seriously that we can best come to see what is wrong with luck egalitarianism. Although there are in theory indefinitely many premises from which the two conjuncts of luck egalitarianism might be derived, the leading contender (and, indeed, the only live option) is the primal normative claim that persons are moral equals in the sense that the interests of each are equally important.[9] Thus, to assess the prospects for a successful monistic defense of luck egalitarianism, we must ask whether that primal claim can justify each of its conjuncts. However, when we do, we find that the primal claim does not really support either a view with the conjunctive structure of luck egalitarianism or the attitudes toward contingency and choice that that view embodies.

Here again, my reasoning must await the argument that follows; but here again, too, I can offer a brief summary of what I am going to say. To get a grip on what the moral equality of persons can tell us about distributive justice, I will begin by trying to identify the facts about persons in virtue of which they *are* moral equals. Identifying these facts is often said to be problematic because people differ along

---

[9] Thomas Nagel, who endorses a version of luck egalitarianism in his book *Equality and Partiality* (Oxford University Press, 1991), gestures at the idea that it is grounded in the moral equality of persons when he writes that "if everyone matters just as much as everyone else, it is appalling that the most effective social systems we have been able to devise permit so many people to be born into conditions of harsh deprivation which crush their prospects for leading a decent life, while many others are well provided for from birth" (p. 64). In *Sovereign Virtue*, Ronald Dworkin explicitly presents his distributive account as resting on (a version of) the view that all persons are owed equal concern.

every empirical dimension; but I will argue that this objection misses the point because the crucial fact about persons is not empirical at all. It is, rather, that each person has a subjective perspective that is uniquely his own. Although no two people have the same combination of abilities, physical traits, and psychological propensities, each is equally a complete and self-contained center of thoughts, feelings, and experiences. It is, I will argue, precisely the fact that we are equals in this respect — that each is a world unto himself — that best explains why each person's interests are of equal moral importance.

Because our internal lives are inaccessible to others, they do not lend themselves to empirical investigation. Nevertheless, because we have compelling indirect evidence that each person's subjectivity is organized around the same fundamental assumptions (about, for example, the spatial and temporal structure of the world, the efficacy of his decisions, the availability of theoretical and practical reasons, and so on), it remains possible to generalize about the interests to which the structure of our subjectivity gives rise. In particular, because each person's consciousness is by nature oriented toward assessing the available reasons and forming beliefs and acting on the basis they provide, it is plausible to maintain that each person's most fundamental interest consists of successfully performing just these activities. It consists, in other words, of actively living his own life in whichever way he thinks best. Although our judgments about our reasons give rise to innumerable more specific interests, these are subordinate to, and hence less fundamental than, our overarching interest in living our own lives in our own way. And because a just society must attach equal weight to each member's fundamental interest — this is just the social version of the primal normative claim — it follows that a just society must give each of its members an equal *chance* to live his own life in his own way.

Although I have so far said nothing about the *distribution* of goods among persons, this proposal can easily be reformulated in distributive terms. To do so, we need only introduce a good that corresponds to what I have identified as our most fundamental interest: the good, roughly, of being able to live one's own life effectively. Although this good is (even) more abstract than such familiar goods as welfare, resources, opportunities, and capabilities, its distribution among a society's members is no less a function of the society's important institutions. And, in view of this, the proposal I have just advanced — that a just society must give each of its members an equal chance to live his life as he thinks best — will go over smoothly into the claim that a just society must distribute equally among its members the abstract good of being able to live their lives effectively.

III

Is it possible to derive both conjuncts of luck egalitarianism from the primal normative claim that persons are moral equals? At first glance, the answer may appear to be "yes." I have just suggested that the moral equality of persons calls for the equal distribution of a certain abstract good — the ability to live one's life effectively — which in turn is intimately bound up with the ability to make and implement reason-based choices. If the inegalitarian effects of people's choices were systematically thwarted — if the predictable consequences of those choices were blocked whenever allowing them to play themselves out would leave some better off than others — then people would exercise little real control over their lives. Thus, in any society whose members *are* able to live their lives effectively, the differences in what the parties choose are bound to lead to significant inequalities of welfare, resources, and opportunities. In addition, because a person's ability to live his life effectively depends in part *on* his level of resources and opportunities, the resulting differences in resources and opportunities can sometimes be expected to disrupt the equal distribution of that ability itself.

Because the claim that persons are moral equals thus supports a form of distributive equality which in turn leads to various distributive *in*equalities, that claim may appear to establish precisely the kind of internal connection between the two conjuncts of luck egalitarianism that the monist is seeking. However, on closer inspection, it does not; for neither main variant of the view that emerges has the same structure as luck egalitarianism. To see this, let us briefly examine each variant in turn.

Consider first the variant which asserts that because justice requires that persons be rendered equally able to live their lives effectively, it must also endorse whichever inequalities of welfare, resources, and opportunities arise through that ability's differential exercise. Put most simply, the reason this variant is not a version of luck egalitarianism is that the good whose equal distribution is called for by its first clause is not the same as the one whose unequal distribution is sanctioned by its second. Despite their disagreements about what Gerald Cohen has called the currency of distributive justice, all luck egalitarians agree that justice *has* a single currency, and that the unequal distribution of whatever good comprises it is just when it results from the parties' choices but unjust when it does not. By contrast, what the current claim asserts is that there is one sort of good (the ability to live one's life effectively) whose unequal distribution is unjust, period, but that precisely because of this there are various other goods, such as resources and welfare, whose unequal distribution *is* just as long as *it* stems from choice. Where the most fundamental good is concerned, this claim demands equality without exception, while where less fundamental goods are concerned, it allows inequality in accordance with choice. Thus, when we draw out the distributive implications of the moral equality of persons in this way, what we get is not a pair of conjuncts that exhaustively determine the distribution of a single crucial good, but rather a single principle that governs the crucial good and a number of subordinate principles, governing others, that follow from it. Even if this proposal is expressed in conjunctive terms, its conjuncts will remain stratified in a way that those of luck egalitarianism are not.

Consider next the variant which asserts that because societies must render their members equally able to live their lives effectively, they must allow people's choices to play themselves out in ways which sometimes lead to inequalities *in the distribution of that very ability*. Unlike its predecessor, this variant does not assert merely that the equal distribution of one type of good rules out the equal distribution of another. Instead, no less than luck egalitarianism itself, it focuses on a single good throughout. However, when luck egalitarians maintain that inequalities are just if they reflect the parties' choices but unjust otherwise, they are merely asserting a biconditional which in itself calls neither for equality nor for inequality. By contrast, when I say that justice requires the equal distribution of an abstract ability whose exercise in turn causes it to be unequally distributed, I am making a claim which simultaneously calls for both. There are obvious questions about how we can best resolve this tension, but I need not go into these here. Instead, for now, the point is simply that this second variant of my view is no less structurally different from the standard versions of luck egalitarianism than is the first.

IV

If my account differed from luck egalitarianism only in the underlying structure of its claims, but not in what it implies about which inequalities of welfare, resources, or opportunities are just and which unjust, then the difference would be of merely theoretical interest. However, in fact, the structural differences ramify widely, and the two accounts have very different substantive implications. To bring these into the open, it will be helpful to contrast the roles that contingency plays in the two accounts.

To the luck egalitarian, luck and contingency – we can for present purposes treat them as interchangeable – play a purely negative role. They are defined purely in terms of the absence of choice, and the inequalities to which they give rise are viewed merely as obstacles for justice to overcome. Whenever an inequality in two people's levels of resources or well-being can be traced to what is, from the parties' own standpoint, an uncontrollable contingency – whenever, for example, the reason one person has more than another is that he was born with a talent that is more in demand, has received a better education, or has remained healthy while the other got sick – the luck egalitarian will view the resulting inequality as unjust, and hence will seek its elimination. Under luck egalitarianism, contingency is the enemy of justice.

By contrast, if we subordinate the distribution of resources and well-being to the more basic requirement that all persons be rendered equally able to live their own lives effectively, then contingency will play a different and far more positive role; for living one's life effectively consists precisely of coping effectively with the unique and ever-changing challenges and opportunities that happenstance throws up. Of the contingencies that shape our lives, some are positive, as when we meet someone who will turn out to be important to us because we happen to be in the right place at the right time, but many others are negative. We all have personal limitations of which we are keenly aware, we are all subject to rejection, setbacks, disappointment, and loss, and we all encounter sickness and other forms of unpleasantness that no infusion of resources can prevent. Although illnesses, career setbacks, and bad marriages are undeniably harder to deal with when we lack adequate medical care or have nagging worries about paying the rent, they are, once these needs are met, strikingly resistant to manipulation by others. The challenges they pose are ones we must face for ourselves, and our responses to them are the stuff of which our lives are made.

When it is viewed from this perspective, the project of eliminating all unchosen inequalities can be seen to be both futile and self-defeating. That project is futile because of the sheer immensity and variety of the factors that would have to be evened out, while it is self-defeating because if (impossibly) it were realized, the lives that remained open to persons would be so deracinated as to lose much of their moral importance. We have a name for situations in which different individuals try to advance their interests in structured situations that give none an advantage – they're called games – and while games are often a needed respite from the messy business of living, they are hardly a substitute for it.[10] Thus, far from impeding the ability whose equal distribution among persons is primarily in question, the innumerable contingencies that differ from person to person are a necessary condition for its exercise.

From any given agent's perspective, both the economic system under which he lives and the past events that have shaped his position

---

[10] When contingency is understood in this way, there remains a sense in which it is the complement of choice; but the sense in which this is so is not that choice and contingency are mutually exclusive, but rather that contingency alone provides the backdrop against which choices become meaningful.

within it are simply fixed features of his situation. In this respect, a person's economic circumstances are no different from the innumerable other contingencies his responses to which determine the effectiveness with which he lives his life. Moreover, just as someone who is born with a handicap, or whose marriage has gone hopelessly sour, may nevertheless be able to live his life effectively, so too may someone of modest economic means. Because my proposal asserts that it is equality in this more abstract dimension that matters for justice, its account of justice is compatible not only with many economic inequalities that issue *from* the parties' choices, but also with some that exist prior to choice and that shape the options among which the parties' choices are made. The account's acceptance of this additional class of economic inequalities is among the most important respects in which its substantive implications differ from those of luck egalitarianism.

Just how great the difference turns out to be will depend on various factors, the most obvious of which is the exact content of the idea of living one's life effectively. That is obviously something I will have to say a lot more about. However, for now, the point is simply that although my account does not condemn all unchosen inequalities of wealth, it also does not give them all its blessing. Even if the account implies that a measure of adaptive preference formation on the part of the economically worse-off is consistent with justice – and I think, in fact, that it does imply this – it will also imply that there are certain levels of wealth and opportunity that a person must have in order to live *any* sort of life effectively. These levels are determined, in part, by the obvious facts that those who are desperately poor cannot look beyond their immediate needs, cannot reasonably make or pursue long-term plans, and have few opportunities to shape their own destinies. They are determined, as well, by the many more subtle ways in which social and economic hierarchies undermine the efforts, and blight the prospects, of the less well off. If some members of a society fall below the relevant levels while others exceed them, then that society's arrangements will be no less unjust under my account than they are under luck egalitarianism.

V

This way of reconciling the demands of equality and choice provides a new perspective on a variety of familiar debates. It illuminates both the debate about whether the currency of distributive justice is best understood as welfare, resources, opportunities, primary goods, capabilities, or something else and the three-cornered dispute among egalitarians, prioritarians, and those who favor some form of sufficiency. Moreover, although these debates are often conducted in relative isolation from one another, the proposed account allows us to connect them in an easy and natural way.

For if the fundamental distributive aim is to render each person equally able to live his own life effectively, then the significance of resources, opportunities, and the rest will lie precisely in their utility in advancing that aim. This gives us a purchase on the way in which each such good should be distributed. Because I have suggested that living one's life effectively involves adjusting one's ends to the available means, it should already be clear that I take the principle that ought to govern the distribution of wealth and resources to be sufficiency rather than equality or priority. Moreover, although the details vary, I will argue that something similar holds for each other entry on the list. Because my account thus implies that what is important about each good is only that each agent have enough of it to be able to live his life effectively, it eliminates the need to establish which good takes precedence when, for example, distributing resources equally would lead to inequalities in welfare and vice versa. As long as everyone has enough of each good, we need not press for equality in the distribution of either.

One standard criticism of the sufficiency view is that there is no non-arbitrary way to specify how much of any good is enough. However, on the account that I will defend, each relevant threshold is established by the requirement that each person be able to live his life effectively. Moreover, as we will see, the content of that requirement is in turn determined by the standards of success that are internal to the activities into which our consciousness channels us. Because both the nature of those activities and the standards that they incorporate are subject to different interpretations, this is not the kind of argument that will allow us to draw a bright line between the amounts of any good that are and are not sufficient. Nevertheless, by drilling down into the considerations that ground our moral equality, we can at least arrive at a principled way of thinking about the sufficiency threshold for each good on the standard list.

Because welfare, resources, and opportunities all stand in different relations to the ability to live one's life effectively, each such threshold is independent of the others, and each raises its own set of issues. Thus, on the one hand, because the effectiveness with which a person is able to live his life is largely independent of how happy he is, the threshold that determines the amount of subjective well-being to which individuals may lay claim against their society is on my account very low. Indeed, the only reason to speak of a threshold here at all is that one of the factors that can prevent someone from being able to live his life effectively is the kind of debilitating depression that can sometimes be mitigated through treatment. By contrast, because wealth, resources, and opportunities are all goods on which people draw in the course of living their lives – because they are all in this sense instrumental goods – the question of how much of each a person needs to live his life effectively is one that has real weight. Assuming commensurability of thresholds, we can expect the thresholds that determine the minimal acceptable amounts of these goods to be set considerably higher than the one that determines the minimum acceptable amount of welfare. Moreover, although the issues are different again, the same holds for some (though not all) of the capabilities for functioning upon which Amartya Sen and Martha Nussbaum focus.[11] In particular, because literacy and the different forms of practical and theoretical rationality are so closely bound up

---

[11] Sen has argued in many places that theories of justice should focus primarily on capabilities for functioning; see, for example, Amartya Sen, "Equality of What?" in *The Tanner Lectures on Human Values*, ed. Sterling McMurrin (Cambridge University Press, 1980), and Amartya Sen, *Inequality Reexamined* (Oxford University Press, 1992). For an overview of Nussbaum's position that contains a list of the capabilities that she views as minimally necessary for a flourishing life, see

with the ability to live one's life effectively, the case for equalizing that ability will turn out to have important implications about the minimum acceptable amounts of these capabilities.

To make the suggestions of the foregoing paragraph precise, I will obviously have to look more carefully at the relation between each of the cited goods and the fundamental ability whose equal distribution is in question. However, in addition, I will have to address the more general problem that even people who are able to live their lives effectively often make a mess of things, and that a person's bad choices can easily move him from a position above one of the relevant thresholds to a position below it. Because such shifts can occur, I must explain *when* in a person's life the relevant thresholds must be met. Must he have sufficient resources, opportunities, and capabilities at all points in his life, or only at some? And, if only some, then which?

From my claim that no one can live his life effectively unless the predictable consequences of his choices are allowed to play themselves out, it may seem to follow that each threshold must be reached only at some early point in a person's life – that the only time at which it is unjust for someone to have less than a sufficient amount of resources, opportunities, or capabilities is when he reaches the age of majority, or what Dworkin calls "the starting gate."[12] However, in fact, the issue is not this simple; for because most of a person's life is lived after he leaves the starting gate, its overall effectiveness cannot depend exclusively on his initial choices. Despite the temporal priority of those choices, the ones he makes later must also matter, and so too, therefore, must his subsequent levels of resources, opportunities, and the rest. This suggests that the thresholds that govern the distribution of these goods must have a diachronic dimension, and that the best way for the state to promote its citizens' fundamental interest may be to maintain arrangements that generally do allow them to bear the adverse consequences of their own choices, but that somehow prevent or mitigate the worst self-inflicted harms in order to preserve their

Martha Nussbaum, *Creating Capabilities: The Human Development Approach* (Cambridge, MA: Harvard University Press, 2011): the list appears on pp. 33–34.
[12] For Dworkin's discussion of this idea, see *Sovereign Virtue*, pp. 87–89.

ability to live effectively in the future. This of course raises difficult new questions, both about how to weight the need to protect the effectiveness of a person's earlier choices against the need to preserve his ability to make effective later ones and about how to reduce the moral hazard that is attendant upon any societal commitment to mitigate the effects of bad decisions.

I remarked above that although my account resembles luck egalitarianism in that each has both an egalitarian and an inegalitarian component, its substantive implications differ significantly from those of luck egalitarianism. I have already mentioned two major differences – namely, that my account, but not luck egalitarianism, (a) assigns a positive role to contingency and (b) accepts the justice of some inequalities of wealth and resources that exist prior to the parties' choices – and I want to end by mentioning two more. Of these further differences, one concerns the inequalities which the two accounts do tolerate, while the other concerns the ones they do not. In each case, my own account provides natural support for a claim that even luck egalitarians want to make, but which they can defend only in an unprincipled and ad hoc manner.

Consider first what has been called "the harshness objection." According to luck egalitarianism, inequalities are just as long as they are due to differences in the choices that the different parties have made under fair conditions. However, even a single ill-judged choice can have disastrous consequences, as when a motorcyclist sustains crippling injuries when he foolishly tries to pass on a blind curve. Because the luck egalitarian formula implies that even a society that can mitigate these injuries at modest cost is not required by justice to do so – or, in one especially uncompromising version, is required by justice *not* to do so – its implications are often said to be too harsh to be credible.[13] Moreover, although luck egalitarians have tried in various ways to soften the blow,[14] it is far from clear that they can

---

[13] For versions of this objection, see Anderson, "What Is the Point of Equality?" and Marc Fleurbeay, "Equal Opportunity or Equal Social Outcome?" *Economics and Philosophy* 11 (2005): 25–55.

[14] See, for example, Kristin Voight, "The Harshness Objection: Is Luck Egalitarianism Too Harsh on the Victims of Option Luck?," *Ethical Theory and Moral Practice*

justify treating the cyclist without appealing to considerations that are external to their theory. By contrast, because my account traces the importance of allowing our choices to play themselves out to our fundamental interest in living our lives effectively, and because it takes each person to retain that interest throughout the different stages of his life, it leaves room for the argument that the cyclist's fundamental interest is not best served by allowing consequences that are this disastrous to play themselves out. By offering an argument of this sort, we can block the harshness objection by appealing to considerations that are internal to the theory itself.

Moreover, just as my account provides a principled rationale for rejecting some inequalities of resources, opportunities, or capabilities even though they are due to the parties' choices, so too does it provide justificatory cover for *accepting* some such inequalities even though they are *not* due to the parties' choices. This, again, is a view that luck egalitarians tend unofficially to share – many are in practice willing to tolerate some degree of unchosen economic inequality in return for great enough gains in productive efficiency – but this acceptance seems merely pragmatic, and appears to involve a retreat from the basic principles to which they are committed.[15] By contrast, because my own account only construes unchosen inequalities of resources or other goods as unjust if they prevent the worse-off

---

10 (2007): 389–407; Shlomi Segall, "In Solidarity with the Imprudent: A Defense of Luck Egalitarianism," *Social Theory and Practice* 33 (2007): 177–98; and Nicholas Barry, "Defending Luck Egalitarianism," *Journal of Applied Philosophy* 23 (2006): 89–107.

[15] Luck egalitarians who explicitly urge the reduction of wage inequality through redistributive taxation while stopping short of maintaining that all jobs should pay the same include Dworkin, *Sovereign Virtue*; Roemer, *Equality of Opportunity*; Nagel, *Equality and Partiality*, p. 114; Serena Olsaretti, *Liberty, Desert, and the Market* (Cambridge University Press, 2004), pp. 162–69; and Daniel Markovits, "Luck Egalitarianism and Political Solidarity," *Theoretical Inquiries into Law* 9 (2008): 271–308. However, for a scheme which seeks to preserve the benefits of markets while eliminating the economic inequalities to which they lead, see Joseph Carens, *Equality, Moral Incentives, and the Market: An Essay in Utopian Politico-Economic Theory* (University of Chicago Press, 1981). For critical discussion of Carens's proposal, see David Miller, *Market, State, and Community: Theoretical Foundations of Market Socialism* (Oxford University Press, 1989), pp. 153–56.

from living their lives effectively, it allows us to say that many of the unchosen economic inequalities that are conducive to efficiency are fully compatible with justice. Moreover, unlike Rawls's theory, which also construes some unchosen economic inequalities as just but restricts them to inequalities that increase the economic prospects of the worst-off, my own proposal involves no such restriction. Thus, here again, my account provides a principled justification for a claim that most luck egalitarians are willing to accept, but which they must view as a compromise with injustice.

VI

As this brief overview suggests, the argument of this book is partly critical and partly constructive. By taking as my starting point the problems that arise when we examine various luck egalitarian attempts to reconcile equality with choice, I gradually work my way to the alternative described above. Here, by chapter, is how the argument will run.

In the three chapters that follow this one, I set the stage for my positive account by explaining what I take to be wrong with the main defenses of luck egalitarianism, both pluralistic and monistic, that can be extracted from the writings of its proponents. Thus, in Chapter 2, I examine the possibility of grounding the inegalitarian conjunct of luck egalitarianism in some free-standing principle or value which requires that persons be allowed to exercise control over their own lives, while in Chapter 3 I ask whether we might instead ground that conjunct in some appeal to the requirements of either responsibility or desert. Although each argument has some initial appeal, I argue that none stands up to careful examination. Then, propelled by the failure of the major pluralistic arguments, I turn to the only well-worked-out monistic alternative – namely, Ronald Dworkin's original defense of a view with the relevant conjunctive structure. Despite the flood of commentary and criticism it has engendered, Dworkin's version of the monistic approach remains the standard-setter. However, I argue in Chapter 4 that it is marred by its inattention to the theoretical basis of its allegedly unifying notion of equal concern. Taking my cue from this, I ask, in the pivotal Chapter 5, what facts about us might support the familiar claim that all persons have equal moral standing. As suggested above, my answer is that we owe our moral equality to the fact that each of us occupies a distinct subjectivity that is structured by the same set of basic assumptions.

From this new starting point, I move in a series of stages to my constructive account. In Chapter 6 I invoke the facts in virtue of which we are moral equals to establish, first, that each person has a fundamental interest in being able to live his life effectively; second, that justice calls for social arrangements that provide each citizen with a sufficient (and, I will later add, an equal) amount of that ability; and, third, that achieving equality at this level means accepting a variety of choice-related inequalities at others. In Chapter 7, I further unpack the notion of living one's life effectively by highlighting the degree to which it consists precisely of coping with an unending sequence of contingencies that no society can hope to tame. In Chapter 8, I argue for sufficiency in the distribution of such important subsidiary goods as resources, opportunity, and education, and I discuss the factors that bear on the threshold for each. In the concluding Chapter 9, I complete the transition from sufficiency to equality in the distribution of the fundamental ability to live one's life effectively, and I return to the question of when a person's earlier exercises of that ability should be allowed to undermine his having it at a later time. Although the principles that emerge from these discussions are too abstract to support many specific policy prescriptions, they do, I hope, provide a framework within which questions of policy may usefully be addressed.

CHAPTER 2

Luck as the absence of control

Why, exactly, should inequalities that are due to luck be thought to be less defensible than ones that are not? This is the central question that luck egalitarianism raises, and it has both an analytical and a normative dimension. The question is partly analytical because we cannot answer it without offering a more precise specification of the feature that separates the two classes of inequalities, but it is partly normative because it also requires an explanation of that feature's moral importance. In this chapter and the next, I will discuss the three most plausible sets of answers to the central question. Because each set invokes the relevant normative consideration only to justify those inequalities that display the cited feature, but not to make the case for equality in its absence, each justification of luck egalitarianism that emerges will be pluralistic. By coming to understand why each such justification fails, we will begin the monistic turn that will ultimately propel us beyond luck egalitarianism.

I

At first glance, the task of giving content to the luck egalitarian's central distinction may not seem particularly difficult; for when luck egalitarians summarize their position, they tend to do so in strikingly similar terms. To characterize the inequalities that they are willing to accept – the ones that are *not* matters of luck – they standardly describe them as inequalities for which the parties are *responsible*. Along these lines, we often encounter assertions such as the following:

What seems bad is not that people should be unequal in advantages or disadvantages generally, but that they should be unequal in the advantages and disadvantages for which they are not responsible.[1]

[The purpose of egalitarianism] is to eliminate *involuntary disadvantage*, by which I (stipulatively) mean disadvantages for which the sufferer cannot be held responsible, since it does not appropriately reflect choices that he has made or is making or would make.[2]

In the ideal luck egalitarian society, there are no inequalities in people's life prospects except those that arise through processes of voluntary choice or faulty conduct, for which the agents involved can reasonably be held responsible.[3]

Taking our cue from this, we may reasonably conjecture that any normative consideration that is capable of justifying the relevant inequalities will itself bear some close relation to the notion of responsibility.

But this conjecture, though not wrong, is not yet precise enough to allow us to move forward; for it is compatible with a number of different views about what is important about responsibility. By directing our attention to different facets of that notion, we can expect to arrive at very different sorts of justifications of the inequalities for which the parties are responsible. Thus, before we can assess the prospects for a successful pluralistic defense of luck egalitarianism, we must be more specific about the forms that an attempt to ground its inegalitarian conjunct in a responsibility-related normative premise might take.

There are, I think, at least three possibilities to consider; for when a luck egalitarian defends an inequality for which the parties are responsible, he may be focusing on either (1) the control that those parties have previously exercised over their current situations, or (2) the relation in which they now stand to their situations in virtue

---

[1] Thomas Nagel, *Equality and Partiality* (Oxford University Press, 1991), p. 71.
[2] Gerald Cohen, "On the Currency of Egalitarian Justice," *Ethics* 99 (1989), at 916; emphasis in original.
[3] Richard Arneson, "Luck Egalitarianism and Prioritarianism," *Ethics* 110 (2000), at 339.

of their previous exercises of control, or (3) the treatment that they now deserve in virtue of (1) and/or (2). Of these three factors, the first is a condition that is often said to be necessary for responsibility, the second is its essential or defining feature (whatever that is), and the third is a distinct normative fact for which responsibility is often viewed as necessary in its turn. Because each factor is of obvious normative importance, each holds some promise of supporting a convincing justification of the relevant inequalities. To assess the prospects for success, we will have to examine each proposed justification separately; and, for two reasons, the natural place to begin is with the appeal to control.

One reason to begin with that appeal is that control, unlike responsibility or desert, is conceptually linked to luck itself. When we call something a matter of luck, what we usually mean is precisely that it was and is beyond some relevant person's control. This makes it natural to say, with Gerald Cohen, that "the relevant opposite of an unlucky fate is a fate traceable to its victim's control."[4] So if we want to link the luck egalitarians' explicit aim of neutralizing the distributive effects of luck to their equally explicit claim that inequalities for which the parties are responsible can be just, then the natural way to do so is to focus on just that aspect of responsibility – namely, the agents' past or present control over their situations – in virtue of which those situations are *not* matters of luck.

The second reason to begin with the appeal to control is that its central normative claim – that it is morally important for each person to control his own life – enjoys virtually unanimous support. That claim is a fixed point of our moral scheme, and can be seen to underlie many more specific shared beliefs. Thus, for example, virtually everyone finds paternalism distasteful, and the standard objection to it is precisely that there is a strong presumption, if not an outright prohibition, against preempting another person's self-regarding choices. In a more positive vein, many would accept one or more of the following claims: that each person's autonomy is worth promoting, that self-regarding exercises of autonomy are to be respected, and that each

4 Cohen, "On the Currency of Egalitarian Justice," at 922.

person has a right to make his own choices because each person owns himself. In these contexts, "exercising one's autonomy" and "making one's own choices" generally function as synonyms for "controlling one's own life." Hence, if we accept any of these claims, we accept the very premise to which we would need to appeal to establish that the value of control, or the obligation to respect it, can sometimes offset the disvalue of whatever inequalities its exercise produces.

II

Might an agent's previous exercise of control annul or cancel what would otherwise be the injustice of an inequality to which he is party? To mount an argument of this sort, a proponent of luck egalitarianism would have to show that the acts or outcomes over which the relevant form of control has been exercised bear some important relation to the inequalities whose usual status they are said to alter. As a short way of expressing this requirement, I will say that what needs to be shown is how an agent can exercise control *over an inequality itself.* However, giving sense to that notion is no easy task.

To bring out the difficulty, let us first recall a number of truisms about control. In general, we exercise control by making and implementing choices with an eye to influencing future events. Thus, a person's sphere of control at a given moment can extend no further than the actions among which he can then choose and the outcomes that each would have. Moreover, because an act's effects can ramify indefinitely, being among those effects is only necessary, but not sufficient, for an outcome's falling within the agent's sphere of control. Of the further necessary conditions, one is that the agent be aware that the act will have the relevant outcome, another is that he be able to perform some other act that would *not* have that outcome, and yet another is that he be *aware* that he is able to perform some other act that would not have that outcome. Taken together, these necessary conditions complicate the task of explaining what it might mean to say that someone has exercised control over an inequality.

The complication arises because an inequality is, by its nature, a relation between the amounts of some good that two or more different people have, and so is typically affected by the choices that each has made. Of the different parties' choices, each generally affects the chooser's own level of advantage far more than it affects anyone else's. If Jones and Smith have both tried to get as much of some good as possible, then the amount that Jones ends up with is likely to be affected by his choices but not those of Smith, while the amount that Smith ends up with is similarly likely to be affected by his choices but not those of Jones. This does not mean that the inequality is causally unrelated to either party's choices – after all, if either Jones or Smith had made different choices, then the inequality, understood as the relation between the amounts they have, would also be different – but it does mean that an inequality is rarely a predictable consequence of the choices of any single party to it. In any typical case, especially in the large-scale contexts in which questions about social justice actually arise, each party to an inequality has at best chosen his own level of advantage, but has not chosen the relation between what he and others have. And, because of this, the view that luck consists of an absence of control may appear to imply that just about every actual inequality *is* a matter of luck for just about every person whom it involves.

If virtually every inequality is a matter of luck for virtually every party to it, then luck egalitarianism will collapse back into straight egalitarianism. Thus, to give luck egalitarianism a fighting chance, the pluralist who wishes to ground its inegalitarian conjunct in a premise about the moral importance of control will have to understand the morally significant form of control in some different way. Because the source of the problem is the fact that people generally lack control over the lives of others, the obvious solution is to focus exclusively on the parties' control over their own lives. As a first pass at doing this, let us consider the proposal that an inequality is within the control of the parties whenever each party controls *his own level of advantage*.

This proposal is clearly an important step forward. However, whereas our initial proposal made the conditions for an inequality's being within a person's control too hard to satisfy, this one makes those conditions too easy to satisfy. To see why this is so, it will be helpful to consider an example. To keep things simple, I will consider only a two-party case, but everything I say will apply also to more complex multi-person cases.

Imagine, then, that one of our parties, Morey, has acquired 10 units of some good by doing A, and that the other party, Les, has acquired 5 units by doing B. Imagine, as well, that when Les chose to do B, he could instead have acquired 6 units by choosing to do C, 3 units by choosing to do D, but no units by choosing to do anything else. In the example as described, there is a clear sense in which Les *has* exercised control over his current level of advantage, since he had other options which, had he chosen them, would have given him more or less than 5. Nevertheless, because none of Les's options would have allowed him to acquire as much as Morey now has, a luck egalitarian would still classify this inequality as a matter of luck for him. This shows that exercising control over an inequality cannot consist simply of exercising control over one's own level of advantage in it.

To square our interpretation of what is involved in exercising control over an inequality with cases of this sort, we must bring Morey's level of advantage back into the picture. However, instead of doing this by reverting to the view that Morey's current level of advantage must previously have been within Les's control, we will have to do it by taking Morey's current level of advantage to determine the extent of the control that Les must previously have exercised over his *own* current level of advantage. We will have to say, in other words, that even if Les has exercised (some) control over his current level of advantage, the inequality will remain a matter of luck for him as long as his previous sphere of control did not include at least one option which, had he taken it, would have caused him to end up with at least as much as Morey. This formulation contains a potential ambiguity, in that "Les could have chosen to have as much as Morey" can be understood either *de dicto* or *de re*. Understood *de dicto*, it means that Les could have chosen to end up with whatever amount Morey ends up with, while under the *de re* interpretation it will mean that Les could have chosen to end up with some determinate amount which, as a matter of fact, just *is* the amount that Morey will end up with. However, because we are seeking an account that will apply even to inequalities the parties to which are not aware of one another's existence, and therefore cannot direct their choices at their positions relative to each other, it must be the second, *de re* interpretation that is correct.

Even as refined, this account of what it is to exercise control over an inequality will not satisfy all luck egalitarians. Against it, some are bound to object that even if Les's not having as much as Morey in fact has can be traced in the relevant way to Les's previous choices, the inequality as a whole is still a matter of luck as long as Morey's level of advantage cannot also be traced to *his* previous choices. In addition, even if this further condition is met, some will continue to consider the inequality a matter of luck as long as the actions that Les would have had to perform in order to acquire the amount that Morey now has were markedly harder, or markedly less pleasant, than the ones that Morey himself had to perform.[5] To amend our proposal to accommodate the first objection, we would have to explain how much control, and what sort of control, the more advantaged party to an inequality must previously have exercised over his current situation; while to amend it to accommodate the second, we would have to specify the respects in which, and the degrees to which, the options of the two parties must have been comparable. However, because no amendment of either sort seems likely to affect the argument I intend to make, I will not pursue these complications, but, having flagged them, will simply leave them unresolved.

III

To justify the inequalities that luck egalitarians accept by invoking the moral importance of control, a pluralist must specify both the form

---

[5] This objection can take either of two forms. Of those who mount it, some will construe the difficulty or unpleasantness of what Les would have had to do to get 10 as having deprived him of (full) control over the ensuing inequality, while others will construe it as a constituent element *of* that inequality. The act's difficulty or unpleasantness will enter in the first way if the point of introducing it is to show that no one in Les's situation could reasonably be expected to perform the act that would have given him 10 instead of 5, while it will enter in the second way if it is introduced to show that Les's overall package of action-plus-outcome options was worse than Morey's.

of control that he has in mind and his reasons for believing it to be morally important. In the previous section, I argued that he can best discharge the first task by saying that an inequality's less advantaged party has exercised the relevant form of control when he has (1) made a choice that he correctly expected to cause him to have as much as he now does, while (2) correctly believing that he could make a different choice that would cause him to have the greater amount than his more advantaged counterpart now has. But does this way of discharging the first task also allow the pluralist to discharge the second? If he adopts this account of what is involved in exercising control over an inequality, can he also find a defensible normative premise which implies that someone's having exercised such control can render the ensuing inequality just? And, if he can, what will that premise say?

At first glance, this question may not seem hard to answer. As we saw, it is widely believed that each person should be free to make his own life choices. As we also saw, many would justify this belief by maintaining either that it is valuable for people to exercise control over their own affairs or that we are under some obligation to allow or promote this. If a pluralist takes the first tack, he can argue that the value of a person's exercise of control over his own life sometimes outweighs the disvalue of the inequality to which it leads; while if he takes the second, he can argue that the relevant obligation sometimes compels us to accept that inequality. Either way, the inference from the claim that the less advantaged party has exercised the relevant form of control to the conclusion that the inequality can be just may seem straightforward.

But, in fact, it is not; for the argument as sketched is defective in two important ways. It is defective, first, because the inequalities over which agents have exercised the relevant form of control comprise only a fraction — perhaps a small fraction — of those that many luck egalitarians are willing to accept. Also, and even more damaging, the argument is defective because its analytical and normative components do not fit together — because the only form of control that we can plausibly take an agent to have exercised over an inequality is simply not one to which the relevant normative premises apply. Although each objection applies both to the argument's deontic version and to its value-balancing version, I will, for brevity, develop the objections only in connection with its value-balancing version.

IV

To see why an appeal to the value of control can at best justify a limited subset of the inequalities that most luck egalitarians accept, we must begin by reminding ourselves of which inequalities these are. As we have seen, luck egalitarians are generally willing to accept inequalities that are due to differences in the parties' choices. Thus, if a given luck egalitarian takes what matters to be resources, then he will agree that it is not unjust for one person to be wealthier than another because the first chose to enjoy a lavish life-style while the second invested his earnings. He will agree, as well, that there is nothing unjust about one person's earning more than another because he chooses to work longer hours or is willing to do a less pleasant or more dangerous job. And, although the point is somewhat more controversial, I think most luck egalitarians would also follow Dworkin in maintaining that it is not unjust for people's levels of wealth to be affected by the risks they take – that, for example, it is acceptable for those who back risky ventures to profit when those ventures succeed, and for winning gamblers to walk away from the table richer than losers.[6]

Because there is at least a modest positive correlation between resources and welfare, many choices that lead to inequalities of wealth also lead to inequalities of happiness and desire-satisfaction. When this happens in cases like the ones just described, most of the luck egalitarians who focus on welfare rather than resources will classify the resulting inequalities of welfare as just. Moreover, most of them will also accept many inequalities of welfare that are due more directly to the parties' choices – for example, the inequalities that result when one person but not another abandons a career that he finds fulfilling, acts in ways that lead to the breakup of his marriage, adopts a debilitating, dissolute life-style, or commits a crime for which he is imprisoned.

---

[6] For relevant discussion, see Kasper Lippert-Rasmussen, "Egalitarianism, Option Luck, and Responsibility," *Ethics* 111 (2001): 548–97; Peter Vallentyne, "Brute Luck, Option Luck, and Equality of Initial Opportunities," *Ethics* 112 (2002): 529–57; and Michael Otsuka, "Luck, Insurance, and Equality," *Ethics* 113 (2002): 40–54.

And – just to complete the circle – most of the luck egalitarians who focus on resources rather than welfare will also classify as just any economic inequalities that result from life-style choices of the latter sorts.

Given the intimate linkage between choice and control, we may be tempted to suppose that each of the inequalities just mentioned was within the control of the less advantaged party. However, given our account of control, this supposition would be unwarranted; for while we have seen that a person's sphere of control never extends *beyond* his possible choices and their effects, we have also seen that a person's sphere of control never encompasses all, or even most, *of* those possible choices or their effects. Instead, a person's sphere of control at a given moment encompasses only that subset of his possible choices that he realizes he can either make or refrain from making, and only that subset of their effects that he both correctly believes he can produce and correctly believes he can avoid producing. If a given outcome would in fact result from a certain action but the agent is not aware of this, then he cannot choose to perform the action on the grounds that it will produce that outcome, and neither can he choose to perform it despite this fact. In a case of this sort, the outcome will indeed *result from* the agent's choice, but it will be no part of *what* he chooses. Although the choice will indeed lead to the outcome, the outcome will have played no role in the agent's calculations, and so he will not have exercised control over it.

Bearing these necessary conditions for control in mind, let us now ask how many of the choices that give rise to the sorts of inequalities that luck egalitarians typically accept are likely to satisfy them. The answer, I suggest, is "not all that many"; for although it may serve certain theoretical purposes to think of each agent as fully aware of how each available act will affect him, or, at worst, as fully aware of the nature and likelihood of each possible outcome of each available act, the foolish acts that we encounter in the real world are very often performed by agents whose appreciation of their options is incomplete or distorted or blurred. Although muddled choices are especially characteristic of those who live disordered lives, they also account for much of the trouble that the rest of us make for ourselves.

To bring the issue into sharper focus, it will be helpful to introduce a few examples of unhappy outcomes that are the results of people's choices, yet are not themselves chosen. Here are four.

1. *Tattoo*. Whisper, at age 19, has drifted into the Goth lifestyle. Like her friends, she favors studded leather jackets, spiked dog collars, and elaborate tattoos. The one she chooses is an attractive vine: it sprouts from her navel, winds sinuously up her body, extends its leaves around her neck, and spreads up the left side of her face and across her forehead. Because the tattoo is so visible and so permanent, her subsequent employment choices are limited to minimum wage jobs at coffee houses and low-end bars.

2. *Fondle*. Yielding to an impulse, Dr. Rosen, an oral surgeon, fondles an anesthetized patient whom he wrongly assumes to be unconscious. Horrified, the patient files a complaint, and Dr. Rosen's license is suspended for several years. When he regains it, his practice is gone. To make ends meet, Dr. Rosen is forced to become a staff dentist at the Dancing Bear State Prison in California's remote central valley, in the shadow of the forbidding Diablo Hills.

3. *Hothead*. Brooke is a competent employee, but she is a hothead. She frequently thinks others are treating her with disrespect, and when she feels slighted, she finds it unbearable to remain silent. Because her coworkers and supervisors find her outbursts disruptive, she rarely keeps a job for more than a few months. Over time, word of her temper gets around and she becomes unemployable.

4. *Mule*. Whisper, whom we reencounter at age 27, has drifted southward, first to El Paso and then across the border to Juarez. There a recent acquaintance offers her five hundred dollars to transport some cocaine to the US. Attracted by the opportunity to repay some debts, Whisper agrees, but is apprehended when her tattoo attracts the attention of immigration officials. When she emerges from prison she is saddled with a felony conviction that further degrades her already bleak employment prospects.

Because these cases are not described in much detail, it is possible to envision each agent as taking note of, but then deciding to ignore, the possible bad consequences of his act. However, it is also possible, and I think more realistic, to envision the agents as simply not thinking the issues through, and thus as not really registering just how badly wrong things might go. Although there obviously are degrees of clarity, there must be some threshold below which an agent is simply too unclear about the consequences of his act to be able to choose it in light of those consequences. It is true that anyone who lives on this planet must in some sense know that drug smugglers risk being caught and that employers do not want disruptive workers. However, if an agent would grossly underestimate the risk if queried, and if his knowledge is buried so far below the surface of his consciousness that it neither plays any role in his deliberations nor exerts any causal influence over his decision, then that knowledge is just too unconnected to his will to yield any meaningful form of control.

Although each of the cited choices has economic implications, each is more naturally assimilated to the agent's life-style. Thus, it is worth pointing out that disadvantageous choices of a more overtly economic sort are often every bit as muddled. When people impulsively quit their jobs, save nothing for the future, or go on credit card binges, the adverse consequences of their behavior are seldom salient enough to play much role in their deliberations. This does not mean that such persons are not *responsible* for the disadvantages they incur – because those disadvantages are easily foreseeable, I think they clearly are – but it does mean that the choices through which they incur those disadvantages are often not clear-eyed enough to satisfy the conditions for control.[7]

V

So far, we have seen that reconstructing the case for the inegalitarian conjunct of luck egalitarianism in terms of the value of control would mean rejecting many, if not most, of the inequalities that luck

---

[7] For extended defense of the view that agents can be responsible for aspects of their actions of which they were not aware, and for outcomes which they did not expect those actions to produce, see George Sher, *Who Knew? Responsibility without Awareness* (Oxford University Press, 2009).

egalitarians are standardly willing to accept. Even by itself, this would be a serious difficulty. However, as I suggested above, there is also a further and more decisive reason to reject the appeal to the value of control; and to bring this into the open, we need only juxtapose our analytical account of what exercising control over an inequality comes to with our substantive reasons for valuing control.

For consider, first, the content of the analytical account. As we saw, that account says, first, that the crucial party to an inequality is the less advantaged party, and, second, that what we mean by saying that the less advantaged party exercised control is that he made a choice that he correctly expected to cause him to have his current amount while also correctly believing that some other available choice would cause him to have the greater amount that his more advantaged counterpart in fact has now. Although the more advantaged party's having as much as he does is no part of what the less advantaged party has chosen, it nevertheless remains an essential element of the analysis because it provides the benchmark that determines whether the less advantaged party's choices qualify as exercises of the relevant form of control.

Consider, next, our substantive reasons for *valuing* control. These, we saw, are rooted in each person's uniquely intimate relation to his own life. Because your life is your own – because it is you and not I who must live it – we naturally suppose that you, and not I, should be the one to decide what goes on in it. Because the same reasoning applies to everyone, and because deciding what goes on in one's life is equivalent to exercising control over it, we have good reason to believe that it is best that each person exercise control over his own life.

And consider, finally, the relation between these elements. At first glance, they may appear to fit together well, since the substantive reasoning tells us why control is valuable while the analysis tells us what control amounts to in the distributive context. However, on closer inspection, the fit is not good at all; for the substantive reasoning establishes only that a person's exercising control *over his own life* is valuable, while the analysis takes someone's exercising control over an inequality to depend on something that is external to his life.

That something, of course, is the amount that his more advantaged counterpart has, which sets the benchmark that determines whether his choices do or do not qualify as exercises of control over the inequality. But why, if what is valuable is the agent's control over his own life, should the value of his choices depend on what anyone else has?

To bring out the force of this question, let us revert to the earlier example in which the worse-off party to an inequality, Les, has made a choice that caused him to have 5 units of some good when his other available choices would have given him 0, 3, or 6. According to our analytical account, Les will not qualify as having exercised control over the inequality if its more advantaged party, Morey, has 10 units of the good, but Les will qualify as having exercised control if Morey has only 6 units. Thus, if the reason it is important for Les to exercise control over the inequality is that it is valuable for him to exercise control over his own life, then the fact that Morey has 10 units instead of 6 will have to have some impact on Les's life. In actuality, however, what Morey has may well have no impact on Les at all. Even if Les knows that Morey has 10 rather than 6, that knowledge may have no effect either on what Les is able to do with his 5 units or on his psychological state; and, of course, Les may not know it at all. In view of this, the value that attaches to a person's exercising control over his own life does not appear to extend to the form of control that he can exercise over an inequality in which he is the less advantaged party.

This point can be made in another way. Imagine first a scenario in which there is no Morey, and that Les has exercised (whatever you regard as) full control over his own life; and imagine that within this scenario Les has acquired 5 units of a good when he could have acquired as few as 0 or as many as 6. Then imagine a second scenario which is in every way identical except that it contains a Morey who lives hundreds of miles away, who never interacts with Les, and who has 10 units. Does Les have any less control over his life in the second scenario than he does in the first? If, as it seems, he does not, then exercising control over the inequalities to which one is party cannot be a requirement for exercising control over one's own life.

This need not be the end of the story. A persistent pluralist could prolong the discussion by insisting that the bare fact of having less of some good than another person *is* an important part of a person's life. Alternatively, he might contend that exercising control over one's comparative level of advantage is important for reasons *distinct* from the value of controlling one's life. However, neither move seems promising, since the first would deform our intuitive idea of a person's life in a way that diminished the attraction of the claim that he alone should exercise control over it, while the second would dispense with that claim without, as far as I can see, being able to offer a plausible alternative. These considerations suggest that instead of pressing forward with his attempt to defend the relevant inequalities by appealing to the value of the control that the less advantaged parties have exercised over them, the pluralist may do better by grounding his defense in some other principle or value that is associated with choice. To that possibility, I therefore turn.

CHAPTER 3

Equality, responsibility, desert

In the previous chapter, I argued that a pluralist cannot plausibly defend an unequal distribution by maintaining that its disvalue is outweighed by the value of the control that its less advantaged party has exercised in bringing it about. In the current chapter, I will examine two other ways in which a pluralist might defend the inequalities that luck egalitarians accept. Of these alternative strategies, the first is to continue to focus on the parties' responsibility but to locate its moral significance in some factor other than their control, while the second is to turn away from responsibility and argue that the inequalities are justified because they are *deserved*.[1] Although each argument has some initial appeal, I will argue that neither succeeds.

I

The first argument – that what justifies the inequalities that luck egalitarians accept is some aspect of the parties' responsibility other than their control – owes its appeal to two facts. It is attractive, first, because attributions of responsibility have well-known normative implications, and, second, because in practice even if not always in theory, we often do hold people responsible for acts and outcomes over which they lack control. When someone negligently causes an

---

[1] In his article "Justice and Bad Luck" (*Stanford Encyclopedia of Philosophy*, 2009, online, n.p.), Kasper Lippert-Rasmussen observes that luck can be understood as the complement either of responsibility or of desert. Because he also notes that the conditions for responsibility are sometimes, but not always, said to include control, Lippert-Rasmussen's division suggests the same justificatory possibilities that I am proposing.

accident or forgets to fulfill an important duty, his failure to realize what he is doing, and his attendant lack of control, generally does not lead us to say either that he is not responsible for his lapse or that his responsibility does not affect the ways in which we may or should react to him. At most, his lack of awareness may temper the harshness of the reactions that we view as appropriate.

The second argument – that what justifies deviations from equality is that people sometimes *deserve* different quantities of various goods – is if anything even more appealing. We often say that hard workers deserve to be rewarded and that best-qualified candidates deserve positions, and when we do, we clearly imply that there is a sense in which they ought to have these things. Moreover, unlike responsibility, which is attributable only to particular individuals, and so is not ideally suited to justifying inequalities among them, desert has a comparative as well as a noncomparative dimension. Even if we are unsure how much pay any given worker deserves, we are perfectly comfortable with the claim that if Morey works harder and more productively than Les, then Morey deserves to earn a higher wage.

In what follows, I will evaluate each argument in some detail. First, though, I want to digress briefly to consider the question of whether the two arguments are really distinct. This question arises because there is considerable overlap between the outcomes for which agents are said to be responsible and those they are said to deserve. Agents who both seem responsible for their situations and appear to deserve them include persons who have achieved success by working hard for a long time, persons who are now disadvantaged because they have improvidently squandered opportunity after opportunity, and (at least according to retributivists) persons who receive just punishment. This overlap is significant because one way to explain it would be to say that desert and responsibility do their justificatory work in tandem – that, on the one hand, a person cannot deserve something unless he is responsible for it, and that, on the other, what is morally significant about responsibility is precisely that people *do* deserve what they are responsible for. If this explanation were correct, then the appeals to responsibility and desert would not really be independent, and so would best be considered together.

But in fact, the explanation cannot be correct; for we have ample reason to deny both that desert is always accompanied by responsibility and that responsibility is always accompanied by desert. The claim that people can only deserve what they are responsible for is open to objection on both conceptual and commonsense grounds. The conceptual difficulty is that whereas it is perfectly intelligible to say that a person can deserve something that does not yet exist, and that may never come to exist, it is *not* intelligible to say that someone can be responsible either for any action that he has not yet performed or for any occurrence that is not the result of any action that he has performed.[2] Because the concept of responsibility is tethered to the actual in a way that desert is not, the range of things that people can deserve is, in at least one respect, much wider than the range of things for which they can be responsible.

This *a priori* claim is borne out by our reactions to various examples. We can easily find cases that just about anyone who is sympathetic to both desert and responsibility will take to involve desert while not involving responsibility. To envision an agent who deserves an outcome that does not occur, and for which he therefore is not responsible, we may think either of a hard worker who deserves the success that has eluded him or of a criminal who evades the law and so is never punished. Alternatively, to find a case in which an agent deserves, but is not responsible for, an outcome that actually does occur, we can imagine a hard-working, decent person whose efforts to escape poverty all end in failure, but who then becomes wealthy when a long-lost uncle leaves him a fortune. Although such a person would clearly not be responsible for his windfall, his previous efforts and/or moral virtue might well render him deserving of his subsequent prosperity.

Even by themselves, these considerations would establish that the appeals to responsibility and desert are not just two sides of a single coin. However, a further reason to deny this is that just as there are clear cases of desert without responsibility, so too are there clear

---

[2] Here and elsewhere, I mean to use the term "action" broadly enough to encompass omissions as well as positive doings.

cases of responsibility without desert. Unlike cases of desert without responsibility, these cases are not predictable on conceptual grounds alone. However, to find a compelling example, we need only imagine a person who performs a self-sacrificing act – who forgoes a career, for example, or a chance to marry, in order to care for an elderly parent.[3] As long as the self-sacrificing act is fully voluntary, and as long as the agent realizes it will worsen his situation, there is no reason to deny that he is responsible for whatever losses he incurs. However, because his act is morally admirable, he clearly does not deserve the misfortune he brings upon himself.

Even together, these arguments do not discredit all versions of the view that desert and responsibility are intertwined. Although the arguments do show that agents can both deserve things for which they are not responsible and be responsible for things they do not deserve, neither conclusion discredits the further claim that agents can only deserve things *on the basis of* acts for which they are responsible. In defense of this claim, many would insist that even if the criminal who deserves to be punished is never caught, and so never receives any punishment for which he might be responsible, he must at least be responsible for the crimes that *render* him deserving of punishment. *Mutatis mutandis*, many would say the same about the hard worker who deserves success but never achieves it.

I think, in fact, that the connections between desert and responsibility are not even as tight as this, and that agents sometimes *can* deserve things on the basis of factors for which they are not responsible. (Consider, in this connection, an applicant who is best qualified, and so deserves a position, simply on the basis of his superior talent.) However, I also think such cases are beside the point; for even if desert *is* always grounded in acts for which agents are responsible, those acts will always, and their consequences will often, remain distinct from what the agents thereby come to deserve. This is simply a restatement of our previous observation that what a person deserves

---

[3] Similar examples are proposed by Lippert-Rasmussen, "Justice and Bad Luck," and by Richard Arneson, "Luck Egalitarianism: An Interpretation and Defense," *Philosophical Topics* 32 (2004): 1–20.

is often very different from any actual outcome of any desert-creating act for which he is responsible: recall the self-sacrificing virtuous agent, the criminal who is never punished, and the hard worker who become prosperous through an unanticipated windfall. When desert and responsibility come apart in this way, the demands that the agent get what he deserves and that he retain what he is responsible for having will tell for very different inequalities. Thus, even if all desert *is* grounded in acts for which the deserving parties are responsible, the defenses of inequality which appeal to responsibility and to desert will continue to warrant separate treatment.

II

Let us begin with the appeal to responsibility.[4] When the parties to an inequality are responsible for their positions within it, does this give us a reason to favor, support, or preserve the inequality – a reason that is, on at least some occasions, strong enough to outweigh or cancel whatever reasons tell against it? If so, in what principle, value, or other consideration might that reason be grounded?

At first glance, the obvious candidate is the requirement that we treat all persons as responsible agents. That we accept such a requirement, and that it imposes stringent constraints on our interactions with others, is beyond dispute. Those constraints include a strong presumption, if not an outright prohibition, against the standard forms of paternalism – that is, against treatment that coerces or deceives others with the aim of advancing, or preventing setbacks to, their own interests. In addition, and more controversially, the constraints are

---

[4] Because we have seen that a defense of luck egalitarianism cannot appeal to the moral importance of control, we may be tempted to suppose that a defense whose central normative premise concerns responsibility can only succeed if responsibility does not *require* control. However, although I do think we should reject the control requirement, this inference would be a *non sequitur*. The claim that the defense must establish – that some normatively significant feature of responsibility other than control supports a justification of some inequalities – can be true even if control is also among the necessary conditions for responsibility. Thus, we could accept the control requirement without prejudicing the question of whether some other normatively significant aspect of responsibility can do the job.

often said to rule out various forms of conditioning and manipulation which seek non-rationally to influence either the premises or the conclusions of people's practical deliberations. When we attempt to influence others in these ways, we are said to betray our conviction that they are not responsible for (or are not responsible enough to be trusted with) their own decisions.

But do we also betray this conviction when we seek to eliminate inequalities whose less advantaged parties are themselves responsible for not having more? This is at best unclear, since coercion, manipulation, and the rest seem different in kind from merely preventing people's decisions from having certain sorts of distributive consequences. In favor of assimilating the two classes of activities, someone might argue that because agents standardly make their decisions with an eye *to* their consequences, treating them as responsible must require not only allowing them to make their decisions without interference, but also allowing the predictable consequences of those decisions to play themselves out. However, although there is clearly something to this thought – I will, indeed, rely on a similar idea when I develop my own account – the argument in its current form is a *non sequitur*. From the fact that treating someone as a responsible agent requires allowing him to make his own decisions in light of what he sees as their potential consequences, it simply does not follow that treating him as responsible also requires allowing him to live with the disastrous consequences *of* those decisions. We may consistently hold both that a person is entirely responsible for his self-inflicted predicament and that the only decent thing to do is to help him out of it. Indeed, in addition to being consistent, such claims often appear to be jointly true. Even if one person regularly rescues another from his foolish choices, his interventions, if offered and accepted in the right spirit, need not carry any implication that the other is anything less than fully responsible.[5]

---

[5] In taking this position, I am repudiating an argument that I myself have previously advanced. The argument appears in George Sher, "Talents and Choices," *Nous* 46 (2012): 375–86.

Unlike attempts to prevent people from making disadvantageous decisions by influencing their behavior in ways that bypass their rationality, which often lead to justified complaints that they are not being treated as responsible agents, attempts to limit the damage after the fact neither typically elicit nor typically warrant any such complaints. However, importantly, although a person who is responsible for his own disadvantaged state usually has no grounds for complaint if he is helped, he also has no grounds for complaint if he is *not* helped. If he insists that others are obligated to alleviate his misfortunes, the intuitively powerful rejoinder is "why, when you brought them on yourself?" And, taking my cue from this, I now want to examine the proposal that what justifies (at least some) inequalities for which the parties themselves are responsible is precisely that those parties are *not* in any position to complain.

Unlike the previous proposal, which sought to justify certain inequalities by invoking a principle which purported to govern our behavior *toward* those who are responsible for their own disadvantages, this one rests on a normative premise about those persons themselves. This gives it an appealing directness that its predecessor lacks. However, although the current proposal is a definite step forward, we will not be able to evaluate it until we have resolved a complication that it raises. Put most simply, the complication is that what someone who is responsible for his own disadvantages is not entitled to complain about is not quite the same as what the luck egalitarian wants to justify.

For when someone is responsible for his own low level of advantage, what he clearly has no right to complain about is the fact that he has *only as much as he does*. However, for an egalitarian – and even a luck egalitarian is one – what is unjust about an inequality is not that the less advantaged party does not have more in absolute terms, but rather that he does not have *as much as his more advantaged counterparts do*. Thus, to bring the argument's central premise into contact with its conclusion, we will have to explain why the less advantaged party's responsibility, which typically extends only to his having the amount that he does but not to the others' having the amounts that they do, should also deprive him of the right to complain about the relation *between* the amounts that he and the others have.

To illustrate this difficulty, consider a variant of an earlier example. Suppose, now, that Morey has 10 units of some good and that Les has only 5 units although he could instead have had 10. In the case as described, we may safely assume that Les is responsible for having 5 rather than 10, and hence that he has no right to complain about that; but we may also assume that Les is *not* responsible for *Morey's* having 10. But if Les is not responsible for Morey's having 10, then how can Les be responsible for the complex fact that consists of Morey's having 10 *while* he only has 5? And if Les is not responsible for that complex fact – that is, for the inequality itself – then why, exactly, is he *not* entitled to complain about it?

To answer these questions, and thus to bridge the gap between the argument's premise and its conclusion, we must remind ourselves that it is far from unusual for an outcome for which an agent is clearly responsible to be logically dependent on various aspects of his situation for which he is clearly *not* responsible. For example, when a student fails an exam because he did not study for it, he can be assumed to be responsible for his failure; but even though it would be logically impossible for the student to fail if the exam were called off, or if its threshold for failure were set below the number of answers he gets right, he is hardly responsible either for the exam's being given as scheduled or for the location of its threshold for failure. Or, again – to substitute a positive example – a person may loan a friend the money he needs to meet his mortgage payment, and may thus become responsible for saving his friend's house, even though he bears no responsibility for the foreclosure rules in whose absence his act would not *count* as saving the house. As these cases show and innumerable others confirm, a person's being responsible for X does not entail that he is responsible for all the logically (or, *a fortiori*, causally) necessary conditions for X.

Because this entailment fails, it can be true both that Les is not responsible for Morey's having 10 and that Les is responsible for the inequality that consists of Morey's having 10 while he has 5. And, in particular, both claims *will* be true if the fact that Morey

(or, more loosely, some person or other) is going to have 10 is part
of what defines the options among which Les must choose. Just as
the impending exam and what one must do to pass it were among
the background conditions that defined the student's choice situation,
and hence that determined what he would become responsible for
if he chose not to study, so too may the fact that Morey will end
up with 10 be among the background conditions that define Les's
choice situation, and that therefore determine what he will become
responsible for by making a choice that leaves him with 5 rather than
10. It is of course true that the future situations of others cannot
be part of a person's choice situation unless he knows, or at least
has good evidence about, what they will be. However, because most
people have a pretty good idea of how society's important goods are
distributed, we may plausibly take Les to be aware that many others
(even if not Morey in particular) will end up with more than he does
if his choice nets him only 5. Thus, although complications certainly
remain, it does not seem unreasonable to conclude that the great
majority of those who have forgone choices that would have allowed
them to have as much as others are responsible not only for having
the amounts that they do, but also for the inequalities that separate
them from their more advantaged counterparts.[6]

III

Bearing this in mind, let us return to the proposed reconstruction
of the responsibility argument. Expanded a bit, that reconstruction
asserts, first, that when an inequality is unjust, those who are less
advantaged are entitled to complain about it (and others are entitled
to complain on their behalf); second, that when a less advantaged party
is himself responsible for an inequality, his responsibility invalidates
all such complaints; and, third, that his responsibility therefore also
invalidates any charge of injustice that might be thought to *justify* such

---

[6] *Mutatis mutandis*, the same appears to hold for persons who have forgone choices
that would have caused them to have *less* than others. Thus, although the claim has an
air of paradox, it will often be correct to say each of the many parties to an inequality
is equally responsible for it.

a complaint. Because the less advantaged party's responsibility is said to block, rather than merely to outweigh, the case for his having as much as the others, this argument does not appear to be pluralistic in the sense of simply pitting two reasons of differing strengths against one another. However, as long as it construes the considerations that block the case for equality as independent of those that would otherwise support it, the argument will remain pluralistic in the more fundamental sense of relying on two distinct sorts of normative claims.

Should we then accept the argument? The answer, I think, is that we should not; for although it is correct as far as it goes, its conclusion is far too weak to support the inegalitarian conjunct of luck egalitarianism. To see why this is so, we may begin by observing that even if someone who is responsible for an inequality is not entitled to complain if it is not eliminated, we cannot infer, and it is often not the case, that such a person *would be* entitled to complain if the inequality *were* eliminated.[7] This is obvious enough when the party in question is the one who is less advantaged, since the only remotely plausible complaint he could have – that improving his position would fail to treat him as a responsible agent – has already been discredited. It would be an unmitigated good if a sympathetic employer were to offer the gormless Whisper a new job and a new start.

What is less obvious, though, is that the point holds equally well when the person whose complaint is in question is the *more* advantaged party. From the premise that Morey chose to acquire 10 when he knew that Les would only have 5, and that Morey therefore is responsible for having a greater amount than Les, we cannot infer that Morey would have grounds for complaint if Les were given an additional 5. Indeed, simply from the premise that Morey is responsible for having 10 while Les has 5, we cannot even infer that Morey would have grounds for complaint if equality were subsequently achieved through a transfer of goods or by leveling down – that is, if two and a half units were transferred from Morey to Les or Morey's total were simply reduced

---

[7] This objection is essentially a restatement, in reverse order, of the observation that originally led us to consider the current argument – namely, that even if someone is not entitled to complain if another person does intervene to mitigate a disadvantage that he is responsible for incurring, he is also not entitled to complain if no one does.

from 10 to 5. If this last point is not immediately obvious, it is probably because an agent *would* have grounds for complaint if he were not allowed to retain the advantages that he acquired through responsible choices that were rights- or desert-creating – if, for example, Morey were deprived of savings he had amassed by working hard over a period of years. However, a moment's thought reveals that it is the agent's rights or deserts, rather than his responsibility, that would be doing the normative work in a case of this sort. There is nothing comparably wrong with an agent's not retaining the advantages that he has acquired through his responsible choices if those choices were *not* rights- or desert-creating – if, for example, Morey had simply chosen to push a button that he knew would give him 10 and Les 5 rather than a button that he knew would give them both 5.

We are now in a position to see what is unpromising about the current version of the responsibility argument. Put most simply, the problem is that a person's responsibility for his own level of advantage serves only to defuse any complaints that he may have about it, but provides no positive reason for him to have the amount that he does. This might not be a problem if there were no independent case for equality; for in that case it could be argued that even if preserving an inequality for which the parties are responsible is not a requirement of justice, the inequality is still justified in the weak sense of not being *un*just. However, and crucially, a defense of luck egalitarianism will not count as pluralistic unless it holds that there *is* an independent case for equality. This means that if a person's being responsible for having less than another provides no positive reason for him to have less, there will be nothing to defeat whatever positive reasons for his having just as much are provided by the case for equality. It means, as well, that if a person's being responsible for having more than another provides no positive reason for him to have more, there will be nothing to defeat whatever positive reasons for his having only as much are provided by the case for equality. Thus, on both sides, the normative implications of the agent's responsibility will simply not be robust enough to stand up to the competing demands of equality.

These considerations do not make it impossible to defend the in-egalitarian conjunct of luck egalitarianism by appealing to the parties' responsibility, but they do mean that anyone who wishes to do so must abandon the pluralist paradigm. Instead of introducing responsibility as an independent moral consideration whose demands can sometimes defeat those of equality, he must argue that deference to responsibility is somehow built into the very principle of equality itself. That, in effect, is what Thomas Nagel appears to be doing when he writes that the principle of equality "object[s] only to the parties being unequal in goods and evils *for the possession of which* they are not responsible."[8] I think, in fact, that this approach has much to recommend it, and I will pursue a variant of it when I develop my own positive account. However, because the approach would take us decisively beyond pluralism, the time to consider it will be after we have completed our examination of the main pluralistic options.

IV

And that time is not yet at hand, since we have not yet considered the possibility of grounding the inegalitarian conjunct of luck egalitarianism in the fact that some people are more *deserving* than others. Although this possibility has received comparatively little attention, it is, in certain respects, the most promising of all the pluralistic options.

One clear advantage that it offers is that unlike the notions of control and responsibility, the notion of desert is overtly distributive. Desert-claims are by their nature concerned with who should get what, and so can directly conflict with principles of equality. This is perhaps easiest to see when we consider the principle of *comparative* desert; for in one very familiar version, that principle requires precisely that the relation between what different people have be proportional to what they deserve in absolute terms. On this reading, the principle asserts that if in absolute terms A and B each deserve 5, then A should get 1 if B gets 1, 2 if B gets 2, and so on, but that if A deserves 10 while B deserves 5, then A should get 2 if B gets 1, 4 if B gets 2, and so on.[9]

---

[8] Thomas Nagel, *Equality and Partiality* (Oxford University Press, 1991), p. 72; emphasis in original.

[9] Despite its familiarity and intuitive plausibility, Shelly Kagan has argued that this account of comparative desert — what he calls "the ratio view" — is incorrect. For

Because comparative desert can thus demand that different people get different amounts, it obviously can conflict with any version of egalitarianism which requires that they all get the same. However, it is important to realize that a similar conflict would arise even if there were no comparative desert. Even if desert could only be ascribed to individuals one by one, the demand that each person get what he deserves would still conflict with the demands of equality whenever people's absolute deserts differed.

Even by itself, this advantage of the appeal to desert seems substantial. However, a further advantage is that the claim that a person deserves something clearly *does* imply that there is positive reason for him to have it. There is room for disagreement about whether such reasons are rooted in deontic principles or in the value of certain states – I have argued elsewhere that they are sometimes rooted in obligations but that value-reasons predominate[10] – but to deny their existence altogether would simply be to reject desert itself. And because desert is by its nature a source of independent reasons, its reasons can in principle outweigh or annul those of equality. In saying this, I do not mean to take a position about whether they ever do have this impact, but I do mean to say that the question can at least arise.

Bearing these advantages in mind, let us look more closely at the appeal to desert. According to what has become the standard account, the underlying form of a desert-claim is "X deserves Y for Z," where X is the deserving party, Y the thing deserved, and Z the basis of the desert.[11] Within this schema, there is variation in (and, sometimes, disagreement about) both the bases on which people can deserve things and the things of which these bases render people deserving. The features of persons that are said to affect their deserts include the

Kagan's arguments, and the alternative account that he proposes, see Shelly Kagan, *The Geometry of Desert* (Oxford University Press, 2012), Part III. For further discussion of comparative desert, see, *inter alia*, the essays by David Miller, Thomas Hurka, and Owen MacLeod in Serena Olsaretti, ed., *Justice and Desert* (Oxford University Press, 2003).

[10] George Sher, *Desert* (Princeton University Press, 1987), ch. 11.

[11] This schema was originally introduced by Feinberg in his now-classic article "Justice and Personal Desert"; see Joel Feinberg, *Doing and Deserving* (Princeton University Press, 1970), pp. 55–94.

amounts of effort they have made, their performance in competitions of various sorts, their ability to perform effectively in jobs or academic settings, their levels of virtue and vice (as measured either by specific acts or by broader character traits), and their economic contributions to others. The things they are said to deserve on the basis of these features include success and failure at their endeavors, competitive victory and defeat, various forms of recognition and prizes, jobs and admission to educational institutions, happiness and unhappiness, and high and low wages. Of the two variable elements, it is the desert-basis that generally appears to determine the thing deserved.

Given the diversity of these factors (and, we may add, the diversity of the values and obligations to which we must appeal in order to justify the corresponding desert-claims), I will obviously not be able to examine every variant of the appeal to desert. Thus, to keep things manageable, I will restrict my attention to those desert-bases that have figured most prominently in the relevant literature. There are, I think, three such desert-bases; for when philosophers call on desert to justify deviations from equality, they generally take the amount that a person deserves to depend on either (1) his contributions to others, or (2) his efforts, or (3) his moral character. Of these approaches, the first is illustrated by Jonathan Riley's claim that "individuals deserve rewards that are proportional to their productive labors,"[12] the second by Wojchek Sadurski's assertion that "I consider effort to be the principal criterion of desert,"[13] and the third by Richard Arneson's proposal that "what renders agents deserving or undeserving is the degree to which they are steadily disposed to pursue what they believe to be right and good."[14] If the pluralist cannot justify the inegalitarian conjunct of luck egalitarianism by appealing to one (or some combination) of these sources of desert, he is unlikely to be more successful if he ranges further afield.

---

[12] Jonathan Riley, "Justice under Capitalism," in *Markets and Justice*, ed. J. W. Chapman and J. Roland Pennock (New York University Press, 1989), p. 134.
[13] Wojchek Sadurski, *Giving Desert Its Due: Social Justice and Legal Theory* (Dordrecht: D. Reidel, 1985), p. 135.
[14] Arneson, "Desert and Equality," at 272.

V

I think many desert-claims have real normative force, and I see no reason to deny that the demands of desert may sometimes override those of equality. However, I also think that any pluralist who defended luck egalitarianism by arguing that its conjuncts strike a reasonable balance between the demands of equality and those of desert would end by capturing neither that view's letter nor its spirit. To see why, we need only ask what such a defense would imply under each main interpretation of what gives rise to desert.

Thus, consider first the combination of views which asserts that inequalities are justified when they are deserved and that a person's desert is a function of the contributions he has made to others through his productive labor. If a pluralist were to advance this argument, he would have a hard time justifying many of the inequalities that have come about because one person has acted more prudently, or has husbanded his resources more shrewdly, than another. More specifically, he would, among other things, have trouble justifying inequalities that arose because the less advantaged party forwent advantageous opportunities, pursued a debilitating life-style, consumed rather than invested, incurred costly obligations, or took gambles that did not pay off; for when these activities reduce a person's level of advantage, they most often do so not by making him less productive, but rather by depriving him of goods he has acquired by *being* productive (and, of course, in other ways). It is true that someone who leaves school or ruins his health will thereby reduce the value of the contributions he can make to others, but this linkage is at best indirect and is often absent. There need be no loss of productivity when a person incurs heavy alimony payments by leaving his marriage, fails to establish a retirement account, or loses his savings to a Ponzi scheme. Thus, any pluralist who argues that inequalities are justified only when deserved, and who construed productive activity as the only relevant desert-basis, will have to reject many – I suspect a majority – of the inequalities that most luck egalitarians are willing to accept.

We encounter similar difficulties when we combine the pluralist's appeal to desert with the view that a person's desert is determined by the amount of effort he has made. Although people can direct their efforts at any number of goals, those who view effort as the principal desert-basis generally seem to be thinking either of how hard people try in their jobs or studies or of their efforts to acquire the goods whose distribution depends on their performance in these contexts. However, on either reading, a pluralist who maintains that inequalities are only justified when they are deserved, and are only deserved when they reflect differences in effort, will again be unable to justify many of the inequalities that luck egalitarians usually accept. He, too, will have trouble justifying many if not most of the inequalities that arise because the less advantaged party has forgone opportunities, pursued a debilitating life-style, chosen to consume rather than invest, incurred costly obligations, or taken gambles that did not pay off; for just as people who incur disadvantages in these ways are often not unproductive, so too are they often not slackers. Diligence is one thing, good judgment is another, and control over one's impulses is another again.

And, not surprisingly, the same objection will surface yet again if we combine the pluralist's appeal to desert with the view that a person's desert is determined by his degree of moral virtue. The objection might not arise if the virtues that determined desert included traits such as prudence, temperance, and good practical judgment; for a person with these traits will generally not engage in advantage-reducing activities. However, I know of no proponent of the view that a person's level of advantage ought to match his degree of virtue who has actually taken this line, and neither do I know of any argument that supports it. Moreover, of the conceptions of moral virtue that the argument's proponents do accept – conceptions that equate the relevant form of virtue with a steady orientation to the right and good, unswerving benevolence, and the like – none is systematically correlated with a disposition to avoid disadvantageous activities. A person who is unusually benevolent, and is always concerned to do right by others, seems just as likely as anyone else to have forgone advantageous opportunities, pursued a debilitating life-style, consumed rather than invested, chosen to incur costly obligations, and taken gambles that did not pay off. Hence, this combination of views, too, will fail to justify many if not most of the inequalities that most luck egalitarians accept.

So far, I have argued only that a pluralist cannot hope to justify many of the relevant inequalities by combining the desert argument with *any one* of the three most eligible views of what gives rise to desert. However, because exactly the same counterexamples apply in all three cases, my argument also shows that a pluralist cannot avoid the difficulty by acknowledging *all three* desert-bases — that is, by maintaining that some of the inequalities that luck egalitarians accept are justified by the greater deserts of the more productive, others by the greater deserts of the hard-working, and still others by the greater deserts of the morally virtuous. It is of course possible that the pluralist might do better by augmenting this list with yet other desert-bases; but when they are added to the ones already discussed, the standard alternatives — winning competitions, being best qualified for positions, and so on — seem decidedly unpromising.[15]

It seems, therefore, that even a maximally pluralistic proponent of the desert argument will have to reject many if not most of the inequalities that most luck egalitarians accept. Because any complete justification of luck egalitarianism is bound to require some pruning of its proponents' judgments (and because luck egalitarians themselves

---

[15] There is perhaps one possibility that warrants brief mention. In my earlier book *Desert* (Princeton, NJ: Princeton University Press, 1987), ch. 3, I explored the prospects for arriving at a unified account of the normative underpinnings of desert by grounding all desert-claims in the value of autonomy. On this account, the single omnibus desert-basis is the predictability of an outcome from an agent's actions. By claiming that what people deserve is precisely what they can reasonably expect to ensue from their actions, I argued, we can account for the intuition that a person who doesn't study for an exam deserves to fail and that someone who doesn't bring his raincoat deserves to get wet. By extension, the proposal also implies that someone who forgoes opportunities, pursues a debilitating life-style, consumes rather than invests, and so on, thereby comes to deserve whatever disadvantages he predictably incurs. However, for reasons that parallel those I advanced in my discussion of responsibility, I now believe that if it is true at all that such agents deserve the hardships they predictably incur, this is true only in the weak sense they are in no position to complain about them, but not in the stronger sense that there is positive value in their *being* disadvantaged. Thus, like attributions of responsibility, attributions of this form of desert do not give rise to positive reasons for inequality that are capable of counterbalancing those that tell for equality.

do not always agree about which inequalities are justified), this by itself is hardly a knockdown objection. However, my aim in advancing the objection is not merely to show that the desert argument is vulnerable to counterexamples, but is rather to draw attention to a basic luck egalitarian idea (and, in my view, a basic insight) that it systematically fails to accommodate.

Put most simply, the basic insight is that the crucial relation between an inequality and the choices that justify it is straightforwardly causal. Although different luck egalitarians impose different restrictions on the choices whose unequal outcomes they are willing to count as just – they disagree about how equal the parties' options must have been, how aware the parties must have been of their options, and much else – they converge on the idea that when the choices that have given rise to an unequal distribution satisfy whatever restrictions are relevant, *that distribution is justified simply by the fact that it is the result of the parties' choices*. Thus, to capture the basic luck egalitarian insight, a reconstruction of its moral basis will have to explain how the fact that an inequality is a result of the parties' choices can justify it.

Although the value-of-control and the responsibility arguments both fail, each is a recognizable attempt to discharge this task. By contrast, the desert argument cannot possibly discharge it. As we have seen, an outcome can be deserved even if it does not exist at all – a person can deserve something even though he does not currently have it and never will attain it – and so *a fortiori* an outcome can be deserved even if it has not been brought about by anyone's choices. However, if this is so, then even when an inequality *has* been brought about by the parties' choices, this causal relation cannot be any part of the basis on which it *is* deserved. Even if the parties' choices have given rise to the inequality, the causal relation must be incidental to whatever factor really determines what they deserve – incidental, that is, to their respective degrees of effort or productivity or virtue – and so must also be incidental to any justification of the inequality that their desert provides. To say that one person deserves to have more of some good than another is not to attribute any moral significance to the actual outcomes of either person's choices, but is at best to specify what the outcomes of those choices *should* be. Thus, if we want to understand how the actual causal relation between the parties' choices and the ensuing inequality can affect that inequality's moral status, we will have to look elsewhere.

But where, exactly, can we look? Given the inadequacies of the value-of-control and responsibility arguments, it does not seem promising to try to justify the inequalities that stem from the differences in people's choices by appealing to some free-standing principle about the moral importance of choice. Given the inadequacies of the desert argument, it seems equally unpromising to try to do so by appealing to some other free-standing principle. Thus, by a kind of process of elimination, we are left with the possibility of justifying the inequalities by appealing to some principle that does *not* stand free of equality: by showing, that is, that the same considerations that generally tell for equality can also support deviations from it when these reflect the parties' choices. This is the approach that I have characterized as monistic, and we are now, finally, ready to consider it.

CHAPTER 4

The monistic turn

Might a single set of normative considerations tell both for the per-
petuation of those inequalities that do reflect the parties' choices and
for the elimination of those that do not? By raising this question,
we move into relatively unexplored territory; for although a great
deal has been written about equality, the literature contains few self-
consciously monistic defenses of luck egalitarianism. Indeed, the only
two of which I know are an appeal to fairness that can be extracted
from some brief remarks of Gerald Cohen's and the much lengthier
appeal to the moral equality of persons that runs through Ronald
Dworkin's *Sovereign Virtue*. Thus, after briefly considering Cohen's
remarks, I will devote most of this chapter to a critical examination
of Dworkin's position. My main conclusions will be, first, that the
economic inequalities that Dworkin seeks to justify bear no real relation to the agents' choices and, second, that his deeper conception of
equality is too underdeveloped to support any particular distributive
conclusions.

I

In her 2003 book *Justice, Luck, and Knowledge*,[1] Susan Hurley wrote
that we cannot legitimately infer, from the premise that unchosen
inequalities are unjust, that what justice does require is the equal (or
any other particular) distribution of the relevant goods. In resisting

[1] Susan Hurley, *Justice, Luck, and Knowledge* (Cambridge, MA: Harvard University
Press, 2003).

this inference, Hurley came close to maintaining that the two halves of luck egalitarianism cannot be traced to a single normative source.[2] Thus, it is not surprising that when Gerald Cohen responded to her criticism in 2006,[3] he did so by advancing what is, in effect, a sketch of a unified justification.

Cohen developed his response by reconstructing the dialectic through which he saw luck egalitarianism as arising. Within that dialectic, he wrote,

> [t]he luck egalitarian begins by being revolted by what she considers the injustice of actual social inequality. It comes, she protests, from the sheer luck of inheritance and circumstance: it has nothing to do with people's choices.[4]

This single premise, Cohen argued, provides the rationale for both halves of the luck egalitarian position – not only the claim that unchosen inequalities are unjust, but also the further claim that inequalities *are* just when they *do* reflect the parties' choices. Thus, to quote him again,

> [p]ossessed of the premise that luck has caused enormous unjust inequality, the traditional egalitarian proposes, rather rashly, and in the name of fairness: plain, ordinary equality. But now a responsibility objection is pressed against her. Why should one person pay for another's truly optional choices? Since the question appeals to the very conception of fairness that inspired her initial protest against inequality, the egalitarian who rides under the banner of fairness cannot . . . ignore the objection that the question formulates. So, in deference to fairness, the relevant egalitarian says she's against inequalities in the absence of appropriately differential responsibility . . . but that is to say that she's against inequalities if and only if they're a matter of luck. She is against luck *in the name of fairness.*[5]

---

[2] I use the phrase "came close to" because Hurley argued only that the view's rejection of non-choice-based inequalities cannot be derived from its acceptance of choice-based inequalities, but did not take up the question of whether its two conjuncts might be normatively linked in some other way.

[3] Gerald Cohen, "Luck and Equality: A Reply to Hurley," *Philosophy and Phenomenological Research* 72 (2006): 439–46.

[4] *Ibid.*, p. 443.   [5] *Ibid.*, p. 444.

As this passage makes clear, the unifying normative notion, for Cohen, is precisely that of fairness.

But fairness is a protean notion which can itself be understood in a variety of ways. Although Cohen does not make his own interpretation explicit, he clearly takes it to imply that inequalities in the distribution of advantage[6] are fair if, but only if, they are due to differences in the choices made by persons with equal or equivalent option-sets. However, others think it fair that talented and ingenious people be rewarded for their contributions to others and that parents be allowed to bestow what they have earned on their children. If someone holds one of these views, then he will take a fair distribution to encompass many inequalities that *cannot* be traced to the choices of any relevant parties. And, going in the other direction, some maintain that because people are never responsible for what they choose, even inequalities that reflect differences in choice are unfair. If someone takes this position, he may conclude that the only truly fair pattern of distribution is straight equality.[7]

I don't think this lack of consensus about fairness means that the concept is ambiguous. Despite their differing interpretations, I suspect that most would agree that everyone is treated fairly as long as the claims of each are accorded their due weight. However, what does follow is that different people have very different views both about which aspects of a person's situation are legitimate sources of claims

---

[6] As Cohen employs it, the concept of advantage encompasses both welfare and resources. He writes, for example, that "resource deficiencies and welfare deficiencies are distinct types of disadvantage and . . . each of them covers pretty distinct subtypes" (Gerald Cohen, "On the Currency of Egalitarian Justice," *Ethics* 99 (1989): 920–21). Acknowledging the inelegance of the category, Cohen adds that "[o]ne hopes that there is a currency more fundamental than either resources or welfare . . . but I certainly have not discovered it" (*ibid.* 921).

[7] The suggestion that luck egalitarianism may presuppose an implausible libertarian answer to the free will question is advanced by Samuel Scheffler in "What Is Egalitarianism" and "Choice, Circumstance, and the Value of Equality," both reprinted in Samuel Scheffler, *Equality and Tradition* (Oxford University Press, 2010), and by Saul Smilansky in "Egalitarian Justice and the Importance of the Free Will Problem," *Philosophia* 25 (1997): 153–61. For a more hopeful view, see Carl Knight, "The Metaphysical Case for Luck Egalitarianism," *Social Theory and Practice* 32 (2006): 173–89.

and about the relative strength of the claims to which they give rise. Thus, to flesh out Cohen's position, one would have to explain both why people have initial claims to equal amounts of certain goods and why those claims can be modified or canceled by differences in their choices but in no other way. Moreover, to avoid lapsing into pluralism at a deeper level, one would also have to establish that the same considerations that support people's claims to equal shares are also the ones that allow those claims to be modified or canceled by choice and choice alone. These, quite obviously, are simply variants of the fundamental questions that any monistic defense of luck egalitarianism must answer; and because Cohen's appeal to fairness merely reraises them, it does nothing to advance the debate.

II

Although Ronald Dworkin disavows the label "luck egalitarian," his masterful 1981 essays on equality are widely viewed as the first clear statement of that view's leading ideas.[8] Moreover, no less than Cohen, Dworkin takes both the egalitarian and the inegalitarian components of his theory to have a single normative source. However, whereas Cohen represents the fundamental normative notion as fairness, and argues that it tells directly for each conjunct of luck egalitarianism, the structure that emerges from Dworkin's discussion is a bit more complicated. According to Dworkin, the fundamental moral requirement is that each person be treated with equal concern and respect. On the basis of this fundamental requirement, Dworkin argues, first, that each person has a claim to an equal share of his society's resources, and, second, that under the best interpretation of this egalitarian distributive principle, inequalities of wealth that reflect the parties' choices are sometimes just.

---

[8] Ronald Dworkin, "What Is Equality? Part I: Equality of Welfare," *Philosophy and Public Affairs* 10 (1981): 185–246, and "What Is Equality? Part II: Equality of Resources," *Philosophy and Public Affairs* 10 (1981): 283–345. Both essays are reprinted as chapters in Ronald Dworkin, *Sovereign Virtue: The Theory and Practice of Equality* (Cambridge, MA: Harvard University Press, 2000). All page references to these articles will be to *Sovereign Virtue*.

Because Dworkin's position has this more complicated structure, it raises a number of further questions. To elaborate it in a compelling way, he must explain (1) why the requirement of equal concern and respect should have an egalitarian distributive component; and (2) why the goods to be distributed are resources rather than something else; and (3) why achieving this pattern means allowing some to have more than others when the inequalities are due to choice. In what follows, I will organize my discussion of Dworkin's position around what he says in response to these questions.

1. Dworkin's defense of distributive equality is grounded in his well-known view that "[n]o government is legitimate that does not show equal concern for the fate of all those citizens over whom it claims dominion and from whom it claims allegiance."[9] Although he does not quite make it explicit, his argument seems to be that because all persons matter equally, a government's legal arrangements, which profoundly affect each citizen's level of wealth (and thus, indirectly, the amounts of various other goods that are available to him), will not satisfy the requirement of equal concern unless they distribute certain goods appropriately among all citizens. He also seems to believe that because what citizens are owed is *equal* concern, the appropriate pattern of distribution must itself involve some form of equality. Perhaps because he views its conclusion as so obvious, this part of Dworkin's argument goes by very quickly.

2. By contrast, Dworkin's explanation of *which* goods should be distributed equally is developed in luxuriant detail. The two main contenders, he thinks, are welfare and resources, and the clear winner is resources. Because the argument here is far too complex to summarize, I will provide only the lightest sketch of its main elements.

Perhaps the most important strand of Dworkin's case against equality of welfare is his claim that that view becomes implausible and/or incoherent if it takes *all* of a person's projects, preferences, or pleasures (or even all of them that are purely personal, based on good information, etc.) to count toward his welfare. Although the reasons for this claim vary with the version of equality of welfare that is

---

[9] Dworkin, *Sovereign Virtue*, p. 1.

under consideration, they converge on the conclusion that the only projects, preferences, and pleasures that should count toward what is to be equalized are those that do not require an unreasonable share of society's resources. This conclusion implies the normative priority of some version of equality of resources, and thus provides a natural bridge to Dworkin's analytical discussion of that notion. In his view, the only defensible measure of any given person's overall share of his society's resources is the cost that his having that share imposes on others. In its turn, the most accurate measure of that cost is the amount that others would pay for the relevant share. Guided by these ideas, Dworkin proposes, as a model for the equal division of a society's resources, a hypothetical auction in which nothing is initially owned, each individual comes to the proceedings with the same purchasing power, and the bidding for different resources (or parts thereof) continues until an equilibrium is reached and everything is sold simultaneously. After the auction, no one prefers anyone else's bundle of resources to his own, and so what Dworkin calls "the envy test" is met.

3. But, as Dworkin is quick to note, the equality of this division cannot last. For one thing, some people will come to be richer than others because they choose to work harder, invest rather than consume, take greater risks, or have better "option luck" in the outcomes of the risks they take. In addition, some will have talents that enable them to use their resources effectively, and will thus increase their stock, while others, less talented, will use their resources less effectively and so will come to have less. In addition again, some but not others will suffer illness, accident, or some other form of brute bad luck. Although it is sometimes possible to transform brute luck into option luck by purchasing (or declining to purchase) insurance against bad outcomes, this is obviously not possible if insurance is unavailable or if misfortune strikes at an early age. Of the cited destabilizing factors, each threatens to transform the initial situation, in which no one envies anyone else's bundle of resources, into one in which some do prefer other people's bundles.

To defuse this threat, Dworkin advances two important claims. He argues, first, that inequalities that are due to differences in choice do not really conflict with equality of resources, and, second, that equality of resources requires only the mitigation, but not the complete elimination, of inequalities that are due to brute luck. Although these arguments employ very different strategies, they both ultimately rest on the requirement of equal concern, and so are both relevant to the task of explaining how the same normative consideration that tells for distributive equality can also justify exceptions to it.

To reconcile the demand for equality of resources with the inequalities that arise because some choose to work harder than others, to save rather than consume, or to assume greater risks, Dworkin argues that we must broaden both the temporal scope of the demand and our view of what must be distributed equally. On the one hand, instead of seeking to equalize resources at any given moment, we must seek to equalize them over the entire duration of people's lives. On the other, instead of restricting our distributive efforts to whatever resources the world provides, we must also take them to encompass such important aspects of people's lives as their occupations and their labors and leisures within these. Combining both points, Dworkin writes that

> we must apply the envy test diachronically: it requires that no one envy the bundle of occupation and resources at the disposal of anyone else over time, though someone may envy another's bundle at any particular time.[10]

By moving to this more abstract conception of what is to be equalized, we put ourselves in a position to say that people can have equal shares of the available resources despite having very different mixtures of wealth and leisure. In addition, we make it possible to say that people who differ in wealth can have equal shares of resources if one has already consumed what he had while the other has not. Moreover, although Dworkin does not put it quite this way, it seems that taking risks with one's resources lies somewhere between consuming and conserving them. Perhaps for this reason, he also maintains that people who differ in wealth can have equal shares if they have taken similar risks which turned out differently or if they differ in the risks

[10] *Ibid.*, p. 85.

they have taken. Although the inequalities of wealth that emerge as permissible differ in important ways, each is standardly due to some prior difference in the parties' choices. Thus, the resulting theory is said to "make people's impersonal resources sensitive to their choices but insensitive to their circumstances."[11]

Dworkin's other strategy, which concerns the sorts of inequalities that arise because people differ in talent, in health, and in a host of other unchosen contingencies, is quite different. Here the key idea is that a person can mitigate the effects of future brute bad luck by purchasing insurance against it now. Applying this idea at the societal level, Dworkin argues in order to distribute resources equally, a society must insure its members against such misfortunes as lacking salable talents and being born with illnesses and disabilities. To do this, the society must first ask how much insurance the average person would purchase against each form of brute bad luck, and then adopt a rolling scheme of redistributive taxation which exacts from each person an amount equivalent to the aggregate premium and compensates each victim up to the level that the imaginary policy would dictate. By basing our redistributive practices on what the average person would choose, we come as close as possible to honoring each person's choices. Because it would be prohibitively costly to insure against not being able to earn as much as one's society's best-off members, Dworkin acknowledges that redistribution in accordance with this scheme is bound to leave some with less wealth than others. Nevertheless, his considered view, which he adumbrates in a late chapter of *Sovereign Virtue* and makes explicit in his subsequent writings, is that any remaining inequalities are justified by the fact that "equal concern require[s] equality of resources *ex ante*, that is, equality in facing risks, rather than equal resources after risks [have] materialized differently for different people."[12]

---

[11] *Ibid.*, p. 323.

[12] Ronald Dworkin, "Sovereign Virtue Revisited," *Ethics* 113 (2002): 121; see also Dworkin, *Justice for Hedgehogs* (Cambridge, MA: Harvard University Press, 2011), pp. 358–60. This defense of the inequality that is permitted by the insurance scheme appears to differ from a defense that Dworkin advances earlier in *Sovereign Virtue*. In chapter 2 of that work, he argues that a more extreme redistributive policy, which

III

Although a Dworkinian redistributive scheme would significantly mitigate the inequalities that can be traced to brute bad luck, it would not eliminate such inequalities altogether. Because luck egalitarians do reject all such inequalities, Dworkin is on firm ground when he maintains that he is not a luck egalitarian.[13] However, while it is clear enough that Dworkin rejects the egalitarian conjunct of luck egalitarianism, it is less clear that he also rejects its *in*egalitarian conjunct; for no less than the luck egalitarians whose later work he inspired, he professes to accept the justice of economic inequalities that arise because different individuals make different choices under equally fair conditions. Because his professed acceptance of these inequalities is embedded in a broader commitment to distributive equality which in its turn is grounded in a more fundamental commitment to equal concern, it is tempting to conclude that Dworkin has indeed provided a unified answer to our guiding question of how to reconcile the demands of equality with those of choice.

But this is a temptation we should resist; for when we look more closely at Dworkin's reasons for accepting the relevant inequalities, we find that they do not really make contact with the demands of

simply equalized wealth, would affect the incentives of producers in a way that distorted both what they produce and what they charge for it: "if, for example, no one can earn movie-star wages, people who wish to watch movies may perhaps find very different fare available which, rightly or wrongly, they will not regard as highly as what they now have" (*Sovereign Virtue*, p. 105). In this passage and the surrounding text, Dworkin's argument against entirely eliminating the gap between high and low earners appears to be that this would move us farther away from a situation in which each person has an equal share of his society's resources as measured by its cost to others. However, in "Sovereign Virtue Revisited," Dworkin asserts that this was not exactly his point: that the argument of the earlier text was meant "not to condemn postmarket transfers in search of greater equality of resources but only to emphasize that a transfer that makes two people more equal in resources is not automatically an improvement in equality of resources when its effects are fully considered" (p. 122).

13 For Dworkin's reasons for maintaining that he is not a luck egalitarian, see Ronald Dworkin, "Equality, Luck and Hierarchy," *Philosophy and Public Affairs* 31 (2003): 190–98.

choice at all. One way to see this is to notice that there is a large class of inequalities which can be traced to choices made under fair conditions, yet which neither of Dworkin's arguments succeeds in justifying. Another is to notice that even when one of his arguments does justify such an inequality, that argument assigns no real role to the choices of either the more or the less advantaged parties. Let me now elaborate each point in turn.

The choice-related inequalities that Dworkin's arguments fail to justify are those that stem from *foolish* choices – that is, from economically disadvantageous choices which are made not in order to gain more leisure, a more fulfilling occupation, or more of anything else, but simply because the parties are either unaware of, or indifferent to, the losses they will incur. As examples, we may think again of Whisper, Brooke, and Dr. Rosen. In Chapter 2, I represented these agents as acting in disadvantageous ways because they are unaware of the bad consequences of their choices; but it is just as easy to imagine them as aware of those consequences but as momentarily or permanently indifferent to them. When oblivious or indifferent agents act in ways that reduce their future economic prospects, and thus end up with less wealth than others (and less wealth than they themselves would have if they had not acted foolishly), the ensuing inequalities are directly traceable to their choices, but are not justified by either of Dworkin's arguments.

For, first, when an agent makes a choice whose bad economic consequences he either does not recognize or does not care about, the ensuing deficit of wealth is often not offset by a surplus of leisure, by immediate consumption or better working conditions, or by a gain in any other type of resource. There is no reason to suppose that Whisper or Brooke or Dr. Rosen has enjoyed a gain in *any* resource dimension (or even in the irrelevant dimension of welfare) as a result of his disastrous choices. Moreover, because an oblivious agent does not recognize the possibility of a financial loss while an indifferent one does not count it as a cost, we cannot say that either type of agent is taking the sort of gamble that qualifies his subsequent losses as instances of bad option luck. Thus, the first Dworkinian defense of inequality of wealth – that such inequality can be just as long as those with less wealth have more of other kinds of resources – clearly does not apply here.

Moreover, his second defense – that even the insurance against low earning power that persons would purchase in advance if given the opportunity will leave some with less wealth than others – does not apply either. If this is not immediately clear, it is probably because some foolish agents – Whisper may serve as our example – can be expected to be below average in earning power, and thus to qualify for redistributive payments that narrow, but do not eliminate, the gap between them and the better off. However, even in such cases, we may infer, from the fact that the agent with limited earning power *has* made economically foolish choices, that the gap between him and those who are better off is even greater than it would be if he had social insurance but had *not* made foolish choices. At least to the extent that his choices have exacerbated the inequality that the insurance scheme would have left in place, the considerations that justify that scheme cannot justify the gap between him and those who are better off. Moreover, in other cases, such as that of Dr. Rosen, the agent who makes the foolish choices may be well *above* average in earning power. If he is, then he will not satisfy the conditions against which the insurance scheme would indemnify him, and so would not collect anything from that scheme in any event. Because the fact that such an agent has less than others is due entirely to his choices, and not at all to a redistributive scheme that fails to equalize incomes, the resulting inequality cannot possibly be justified by whatever considerations justify that scheme.

IV

Because foolish choices are so common, it is clear that Dworkin's arguments cannot justify all the choice-related inequalities that luck egalitarians (and, I suspect, Dworkin himself) would want to accept. The more important problem, though, is that even when Dworkin's arguments do justify a choice-related inequality, they make no essential mention *of* the parties' choices.

To see why this is so, consider first his argument that economic inequalities are justified when and because they would not be eliminated by the insurance against brute bad luck that the average person would have chosen to purchase if given the chance. Put most simply, the reason choice plays no real role in this argument is that the choices people would make in non-actual circumstances are not a separate and exotic class of choices, as the term "hypothetical choice" might suggest, but are, in reality, no choices at all. When we say that someone who did not know anything about his future life would have chosen to forgo a certain proportion of his income in return for a guarantee that it would never have to fall below a certain level, we are not saying anything about any choice that that person actually has made. Instead, we are merely advancing a (highly speculative) hypothesis about what he would have done in a situation whose description lies just at the margin of coherence.

If this objection is familiar, it is because a close analogue to it appeared in print thirty-five years ago. The context was a critical discussion of Rawls's hypothetical contractarianism, and the critic was none other than Dworkin himself. Discussing a poker game in which the deck is discovered to be a card short in the middle of a hand, Dworkin imagined a person with weak cards suggesting that the hand be aborted because everyone would have agreed to this in advance. Addressing this person, Dworkin remarked that

> your point is not that I am somehow committed to throwing the hand in by an agreement I never made. Rather, you use the device of a hypothetical agreement to make a point that might have been made without that device, which is that the solution recommended is so obviously fair and sensible that only someone with an immediate contrary interest could disagree. Your main argument is that your solution is fair and sensible, and the fact that I would have chosen it myself adds nothing to the argument.[14]

By parallel reasoning, Dworkin argued, the fact that Rawls's principles would be chosen by the parties in the original position adds nothing to the independent case for them.

---

[14] Ronald Dworkin, *Taking Rights Seriously* (Cambridge, MA: Harvard University Press, 1977), p. 151.

And, by parallel reasoning again, we can now say exactly the same thing about the later Dworkin's own claims about the amounts of insurance against brute bad luck that most people would have purchased if given the chance. To justify his contention that a society should not set its guaranteed minimum much above the income that its average member can earn on his own, Dworkin points out that while most people would choose to purchase insurance at a small cost to avoid an improbable but very large loss, most would *not* choose to purchase further insurance at a large cost to acquire a small chance of a somewhat greater gain. When it is expressed in this way, Dworkin's argument invites the familiar question of why anyone's merely hypothetical choices should carry any moral weight. However, that question at least becomes less pressing when we understand Dworkin to be appealing not to what persons in the relevant situation *would* choose, but rather to what they *should*. Despite his use of the language of choice, whatever force his argument has rests entirely on his insurance scheme's rational merits. Like the Rawlsian argument that he criticized long ago, his appeal to the parties' hypothetical choices is doing no real work.

V

My claim that choice plays no role in Dworkin's other defense of economic inequality — the one that maintains that deficits of wealth can be offset by surpluses of other resources such as leisure, past consumption, or fulfilling work — may seem less plausible; for when people end up with different but equally valuable packages of wealth, leisure, and the rest, the reason is typically that they *have* previously made different choices. However, from this fact, it does not follow that their having chosen their different but equally valuable packages is any part of what *justifies* whatever economic inequalities prevail among them. Instead, under equality of resources, what appears to be required to justify economic inequalities is only that each party's overall package of resources *be* equally valuable. So, for example, when a hard worker ends up richer than a slacker, what equality of resources takes to justify the inequality appears to be not that the slacker has chosen not to work as hard, but only that his deficit of wealth is offset by a surplus of leisure whose value to others, as measured by their (not necessarily revealed) preferences, is equally great.

If this reasoning is correct, then choice will play no role in justifying any of the economic inequalities that Dworkin's expansive conception of equality of resources permits. However, before we can accept this conclusion, we must consider a further element of Dworkin's theory that appears to tell against it. That further element is Dworkin's well-known contention that resources can only be distributed equally if people are as free as possible to live their lives as they see fit. If he is right to say this, and thus to maintain that under equality of resources "liberty becomes an aspect of equality,"[15] then it may indeed seem to follow that resources cannot be equal unless each person's mix of resources is one that he himself has chosen. Thus, to complete our examination of the role of choice in Dworkin's theory, we must look more closely at that claim.

Dworkin's reason for maintaining that equality of resources requires liberty is that liberty is a presupposition of the envy test. He argues that the aim of that test – to insure that each person has an equal share of his society's resources as measured by the cost to others of his having what he does – can only be achieved if the prices in the auction that determines those costs are maximally sensitive to each person's preferences and plans. Because a person will bid less for a resource if he cannot use it as he wishes, this means that resources must be auctioned in a form that imposes as few restrictions as possible on their use. For example, land must be auctioned in lot sizes that permit the construction of small homes as well as football fields (or, if only larger sizes are available, then their owners must not be legally forbidden to subdivide). The principle that imposes this requirement, which Dworkin dubs "the principle of abstraction," implies among other things that

> an ideal distribution is possible only when people are legally free to act as they wish except insofar as constraints on their freedom are necessary to protect security of person and property, or to correct certain imperfections in markets.[16]

[15] Dworkin, *Sovereign Virtue*, p. 121. [16] *Ibid.*, p. 148.

And from the claim that equality of resources is only possible against a background of liberty, it may indeed seem to follow that the slacker and the hard worker can only have equivalent packages of resources if each has chosen the package he has.

But, on closer inspection, this does not follow at all; for having the liberty to make a choice is very different from actually making it. It is one thing to say that a society's resources cannot be distributed equally unless its members have enough freedom to make choices that accurately reflect their preferences, but quite another to say that a society's resources cannot be distributed equally unless its distribution has been arrived at through the *exercise* of this freedom. It is quite possible for a person to have the liberty to choose a particular mixture of income, leisure, and occupation, but actually to acquire that mixture in some quite different way. He may, for example, come to have it through his misguided efforts to acquire some very different mixture, by passively drifting into it, or by delegating to some other person (or to his society) the authority to make the decision for him. Despite living in a society in which liberty prevails, a person who prefers leisure to wealth may acquire his ideal combination of these goods not by choosing it, but rather because business is slow and his hours have been cut back. Because it satisfies the envy test, the resulting mixture of resources will by Dworkin's reckoning be equal to the different mixtures of his fellow citizens. Thus, it is evidently possible for an unchosen mixture simultaneously to satisfy both the demands of equality *and* the demands of liberty. Moreover, if an inequality of wealth can be justified despite the fact that the less wealthy party has not chosen to accept less wealth in return for more of some other resource, then even in the more common case in which each party *has* chosen his particular mixture of income, leisure, and other resources, the fact *that* those mixtures were chosen will play no essential role in justifying the resulting distributions.

Might Dworkin block this conclusion by maintaining that even when the equal-resources requirement is augmented by the background liberty condition, that requirement remains only a necessary condition for the justification of an economic inequality? And might he then insist that each party's having chosen his own mixture of wealth, leisure, and occupation is a *further* necessary condition? The answer, I think, is that this move is indeed available, but that the new necessary condition would bear no relation to any of Dworkin's actual arguments. Unlike the requirements that liberty must prevail and that any deficit of wealth must be offset by a surplus of some other resource, both of which arguably do follow from the combination of Dworkin's claim that resources must be distributed equally and his capacious conception of a resource, the proposed further requirement would reflect only an independent commitment to the importance of choice. Because it would not be dictated by the need to equalize resources, simply adding the requirement without linking its justification to that of equality of resources in some less direct way would merely be reverting to pluralism. Thus, if our defense of a theory that allows inequalities that are due to choice is to be genuinely monistic, its premises must differ in important ways from Dworkin's version of equality of resources.[17]

VI

In the previous sections, I argued that neither of Dworkin's arguments establishes that economic inequalities are just when and because they reflect the parties' choices. However, this does not mean that there is anything wrong with those arguments themselves. For all that has been said, the correct conclusion may be that Dworkin is right to say that deficits of wealth are justified if and only if they are either offset by surpluses of other resources or sanctioned by a redistributive scheme that is based on the amount of insurance it would be rational

---

[17] In his recent book *Justice for Hedgehogs*, Dworkin conjoins the requirement of equal concern, which undergirds his account of equality of resources, with the further requirement that government "must respect fully the responsibility and right of each person to decide for himself how to make something valuable of his life" (p. 2). This further requirement does suggest that governments must allow people's choices to play a role in determining what they have; but it is presented not as an implication of the requirement of equal concern, but rather as a separate and independent requirement. For this reason, its introduction does not rescue the claim that Dworkin's way of reconciling equality and choice is monistic.

for each person to buy, but that he is wrong to maintain, in addition, that any just inequality must originate in the parties' choices. It
may be, in other words, that Dworkin has indeed provided a unified
defense of an egalitarian view that embeds an inegalitarian economic
component, but that precisely because of this, we must now rethink
our assumptions about the normative significance of choice.

But before we can draw this conclusion, we must look more carefully at the conception of equal resources upon which Dworkin's
arguments rest. As we saw, he defends the requirement that each person be provided with an equal share of his society's resources as part
of the best interpretation of the more basic requirement that governments display equal concern for all who live under them. However, it
is hard to see how we can assess this or any other interpretation unless
we have some independent grasp of the equal concern requirement
itself. Moreover, because people are so complex, and because they
differ along so many dimensions, there are obvious questions about
which aspects of their nature make them the proper objects of concern,
about which forms of concern the relevant aspects of their nature make
them the proper objects of, and about how they can be alike enough
in those respects to be owed equal amounts of concern. To answer
these questions, an additional layer of argument is evidently needed.
However, despite – or perhaps because of – his repeated assertion
that equal concern is the starting point for all respectable theories of
justice,[18] Dworkin is curiously reticent about what it is about persons
that *warrants* equal concern. Although he is quite forthcoming about
what he takes to distinguish a person from his circumstances,[19] he is
silent both about those features of persons in virtue of which they are
owed any particular form of equal treatment and about the connection
between the relevant features and the form of equal treatment that
they are owed.

There is, I think, a close connection between Dworkin's silence on
these matters and his failure to justify the view that choice can sometimes render inequalities just; for the natural place to seek the missing

[18] For one important statement of this claim, see Ronald Dworkin, "In Defense of
Equality," *Social Philosophy and Policy* 1 (1983): 24–40.
[19] See, for example, *Sovereign Virtue*, pp. 81–83.

justification is precisely in the centrality of deliberation and choice to our mental make-up. I also suspect that greater attention to the nature of the beings to whom concern is owed would shed new light on the relations among the different elements of Dworkin's extremely capacious conception of a resource, and that it would provide him with a platform from which to respond to recent critics like Elizabeth Anderson and Samuel Scheffler, who see our basic commitment to equality as calling primarily for non-domination rather than distributive equality, and who condemn the unequal distribution of goods exclusively or mainly because of the inequalities of power to which it leads.[20] For all these reasons and others, I take Dworkin's lack of attention to the facts about persons in virtue of which they are owed equal concern to be a serious omission.

In any event, my strategy in the remainder of the book will be to try to provide what Dworkin has not. In the next chapter, I will attempt to develop a well-articulated account of the requirements of equal concern (or, as I will put it, of the moral equality of persons) by deriving these from the facts about us that *make* us moral equals. As I have just hinted, our being reason-based choosers will figure prominently both in these facts and in the requirements that emerge. Because those requirements will be said to support an egalitarian theory of distribution which in its turn embeds an inegalitarian economic component, my argument will in structure be very similar to Dworkin's. However, my broader approach will diverge in significant ways, and I want to end this chapter by emphasizing two of the most important differences.

One difference that may already be clear concerns the direction in which my argument will move. Dworkin's strategy is to begin by articulating a comprehensive and attractive account of what justice in distribution requires, and then to rely on its intrinsic appeal to establish that it is part of the best interpretation of equal concern.

---

[20] Two important statements of this view are Elizabeth Anderson, "What Is the Point of Equality?" *Ethics* 109 (1999): 287–337, and Samuel Scheffler, "What Is Egalitarianism?," *Philosophy and Public Affairs* 31 (2003): 5–39. For critical discussion, see Kok-Chor Tan, "A Defense of Luck Egalitarianism," *Journal of Philosophy* 105 (2008): 665–90.

This strategy enables him to tap into various intuitive beliefs about justice, and to draw on a variety of social, political, and economic facts as he understands them, but it limits his ability to draw on his conception of equal concern either to resolve the ambiguities within his theory or to adjudicate its disputes with rivals. My own strategy, by contrast, will be to move in the other direction. Instead of first trying to explain how a plausible egalitarian theory might have an inegalitarian component and then working downward to the theory's normative roots, I will begin by seeking an independently motivated account of our equal moral standing, and will then rely on that account to shape my distributive theory. This strategy, if successful, should provide both a rationale for preferring the theory that emerges to its rivals and a basis for resolving whatever internal questions it raises.[21]

The second fundamental way in which my approach will differ from Dworkin's concerns the nature of the good whose equal distribution is compatible with a measure of economic inequality. As we have seen, Dworkin manages to reconcile these elements by maintaining that the good that must be distributed equally – in his view, resources – encompasses more than just wealth. By insisting on this difference in scope, he puts himself in a position to maintain that equality of resources is preserved when a deficit in wealth is offset by a surplus of another resource. In mounting this argument, Dworkin maintains both that (1) we can reconcile a commitment to distributive equality with a measure of economic inequality by taking the good whose equal distribution is required by equal concern to be related to wealth

---

[21] In adopting this approach, I do not mean to contest the antifoundationalist thrust of the interpretive approach to philosophy that Dworkin defends with great resourcefulness in *Justice for Hedgehogs*. I am in broad agreement with his holistic approach to justification, but I think it has no substantive implications about which philosophical claims can *be* justified. When Dworkin advances his theory of equality of resources as part of the best interpretation of equal concern, he implies that there is something about the idea of equal concern that *makes* the theory part of the best interpretation, and it is natural to seek that something in the nature of the individuals to whom the concern is owed. If an answer can be found, it will of course be just as open to assessment in terms of its relations to our other beliefs as is any other philosophical view.

but distinct from it, and that (2) the relevant good is resources. My own view, by contrast, is that we should accept (1) — this, I think, is one of Dworkin's fundamental insights — but should reject (2). *Contra* Dworkin, I will argue that the good whose equal distribution is required by equal concern is neither resources nor any of its familiar rivals, but is something far more abstract than any of them. *Contra* Dworkin as well, I will maintain that the equal distribution of this more abstract good is compatible not only with the unequal distribution of wealth, but also with the unequal distribution of resources themselves. By adjusting Dworkin's approach just this much, we will be able to preserve what is true and important about his account while arriving at a more adequate understanding of what is relevant about choice and why it matters.

CHAPTER 5

Why we are moral equals

One of the rare points of agreement among moral and political philosophers is that, despite their innumerable physical and mental differences, all persons have equal moral standing (are moral equals, have the same natural rights, are owed equal concern and respect, etc.). There is a significant body of literature that asks which empirical feature of persons, if any, might ground this equality of standing, and a much larger one that asks which principles or policies might follow from it. However, strikingly, these discussions have for the most part proceeded on separate tracks. Here, by contrast, I want to bring them together. By getting clearer about what grounds the equal status of persons, we may hope to learn both why this status requires the equal distribution of any good among them and why that in turn requires the unequal distribution of wealth and other resources.

I

If a given empirical property is the basis of a person's moral standing, and if all persons are moral equals, then it seems that all persons must possess that property to the same degree. This implication is problematic because people vary dramatically along every known empirical dimension. They differ not only in size, age, appearance, health, strength, intelligence, knowledge, and talent, but also in empathy, concern for others, and willingness to regulate their behavior in accordance with shared rules. They do, it is true, all belong equally to the species *Homo sapiens*. However, if this genetic commonality is to be significant, it must be because of the capacities it supports; and these, no less than other empirical properties, all come in degrees.[1]

Not surprisingly, this problem has elicited a variety of responses. Perhaps the most radical is the suggestion that our moral equality neither has nor needs an empirical basis – that it is, in effect, a free-floating moral ideal. In his influential work *Animal Liberation*,[2] Peter Singer appears to advance a suggestion of this sort in support of his claim that the physical and mental differences between humans and animals do not imply that animals are of lesser moral standing. He writes there that "the claim to equality does not depend on intelligence, moral capacity, physical strength, or similar matters of fact. Equality is a moral ideal, not an assertion of fact."[3] If this claim is correct, then the pervasive empirical differences among persons will simply be irrelevant to their comparative moral status.

But quite apart from providing little guidance as to how any goods should be distributed, Singer's suggestion threatens to prove too much. If the empirical differences between persons and cows do not prevent cows from having the same moral status as persons, then the empirical differences between persons and cows on the one hand and trees and rocks on the other will not prevent trees and rocks from having the same moral status either. Singer, recognizing the threat, attempted to block it by pointing out that humans and cows are sentient, and thus have an interest in avoiding suffering, while trees and rocks are not and do not. However, although this response is eminently sensible, it represents a retreat from the idea that our moral standing has no factual basis. The retreat is significant because if an empirical property like sentience can be relevant to a being's moral standing, then other empirical properties may be relevant too. Thus, even if sentience does not come in degrees, some other component of the empirical basis of moral standing – and so too, moral standing itself – still may. Also, of course, it is far from clear that sentience is *not* a matter of degree. It is hardly absurd to suppose that a being with

---

[1] A point that has been made by many. For a particularly thorough treatment, see Richard Arneson, "What, If Anything, Renders All Humans Morally Equal?," in *Singer and His Critics*, ed. Dale Jamieson (Oxford: Blackwell, 1999), pp. 103–29.
[2] Peter Singer, *Animal Liberation* (New York: Avon Books, 1975).   [3] *Ibid.*, p. 5.

a relatively undeveloped nervous system – an earthworm, say, or a carp – is sentient to a lesser degree than a human or an ape.

Perhaps because of these difficulties, most philosophers who wish to reconcile the moral equality of persons with their empirical differences have opted for less radical approaches. One such approach is to agree that a being's moral standing depends on some variable property or capacity, but to insist that what makes persons moral equals is not that each has that property or capacity to the same degree, but only that each has it to a degree that surpasses a certain threshold. An alternative approach concedes that moral equality does require the possession of some empirical property to an equal degree, but allows that it may be what Rawls calls a "range property." To illustrate this notion, Rawls writes that

> [f]or example, the property of being in the interior of the unit circle is a range property of points in the plane. All points inside this circle have this property although their coordinates vary within a certain range. And they equally have this property, since no point interior to a circle is more or less interior to it than any other point.[4]

As should be obvious, the threshold and range property approaches are variations on a single theme – so much so that Richard Arneson runs them together by characterizing Rawls as proposing "that possessing moral personality above a threshold level renders one entitled to the equal basic moral rights of persons."[5]

Both approaches are obviously promising. However, because any relevant threshold must be located on a continuum that is defined by a scalar property, and because any corresponding range property must supervene upon the same scalar property, there are also obvious questions about why we should *ignore* the relevant scalar property. As Ian Carter asks,

> [i]f the basis of a range property is more fundamental than the range property itself, why not concentrate directly on the more fundamental scalar property (or set of properties)?[6]

---

[4] John Rawls, *A Theory of Justice* (Cambridge, MA: Harvard University Press, 1971), p. 508.

[5] Arneson, "What, If Anything, Renders All Humans Morally Equal," p. 108.

[6] Ian Carter, "Respect and the Basis of Equality," *Ethics* 121 (2011): 549.

In addition,

> even if we can justify the moral relevance of the range property when assigning certain goods to people . . . [i]t might . . . be suggested that the relevant comparative assessment of persons ought to be an overall assessment – one that takes into account all of the morally relevant properties of persons, including the scalar properties such as intelligence, sensitivity, strength of will, and so on, on which moral personality supervenes.[7]

In short, although the threshold and range property proposals are both promising starting points, an adequate defense of moral equality cannot merely note that they are formally available, but must provide substantive reason to accept one or the other.

But convincing reasons are in short supply. When Rawls attributes equal moral standing to everyone with the range properties of having a sense of justice and having a conception of the good, he does so because these properties are singled out as significant by the description of the parties in the original position. As D. A. Lloyd Thomas correctly notes, this begs the question by "assum[ing] from the start that variations in degree of rational nature above this minimum are irrelevant to the choice and application of the principles of justice."[8] And Jeremy Waldron also appears to stack the deck against the empirical differences that divide people when he suggests that we focus (exclusively?) on whatever range property best helps us make sense of their moral equality – that, in his words, "the *rangeness* of the [relevant] range-property must match the variability within the human range – i.e. the variability that is *not* so radical as to be regarded as a proper basis for fundamental division."[9]

A more substantial reason for focusing exclusively on a range property is advanced by Carter, who argues that respect for human dignity *requires* that our political arrangements take no account of any empirical differences among those whose agential capacities exceed a basic

---

[7] *Ibid.*, p. 550.

[8] D. A. Lloyd Thomas, "Equality within the Limits of Reason Alone," *Mind* 88 (1979), at 550.

[9] Jeremy Waldron, "Basic Equality," *New York University Public Law and Legal Theory Working Papers* 107 (2009, online, p. 44).

threshold.[10] This ingenious proposal simply sidesteps the problem of finding a factual basis for equality in the political sphere. However, in so doing, it raises hard new questions about *why* the political relationship should be thought to require that we treat our fellow citizens with this form of "opacity respect" (and why it should be thought to require this not only in our face-to-face political interactions, but also in the design of the social arrangements that allocate benefits and burdens among citizens). In addition, and *a fortiori*, there are questions about its extension to moral as opposed to political equality – about the nature of the non-political relationship that is said to call for a form of opacity respect that in turn supports a morality that accords equal importance to each person's interests. Although Carter says much that is suggestive, any thorough examination of his views on these matters would take us far afield. Thus, without arguing the point, I will simply register my conviction that his proposal is seriously problematic, and that the real source of our moral and political equality is apt to lie elsewhere.

II

In his classic essay "The Idea of Equality," Bernard Williams asked whether we can make sense of Kant's idea of respect for persons without accepting his notion of the transcendental subject. This is indeed possible, Williams argued, but to do it we must distinguish "between regarding a man's life, actions or character from an aesthetic or technical point of view, and regarding them from a point of view which is concerned primarily with what it is *for him* to live that life and do those actions in that character."[11] Armed with this distinction, Williams argued that respecting someone requires appreciating and trying to understand his subjectivity. For because "men are beings who are necessarily to some extent conscious of themselves and of the world they live in," it follows that "each man is owed an effort at

---

[10] Carter, "Respect and the Basis of Equality"; see also Ian Carter, "Basic Equality and the Site of Egalitarian Justice," *Economics and Philosophy* 29 (2013): 21–41.

[11] Bernard Williams, "The Idea of Equality," in *Equality: Selected Readings*, ed. Louis Pojman and Robert Westmoreland (Oxford University Press, 1997), pp. 94–95.

identification . . . one should try to see the world . . . from his point of view."[12]

Although Williams was acutely aware of the difficulty of squaring a commitment to the moral equality of persons with an appreciation of their factual differences, he did not explicitly propose his analysis of respect as a solution to that problem. Nevertheless, I think the insight that underlies the analysis is in fact the key to the problem's solution. In what follows, I will argue that it is precisely the fact that each of us is a conscious subject – that each has a subjectivity of a certain characteristic sort – that underlies and supports our claim to moral equality.

To bring out what I have in mind, it will be helpful to consider an objection that Ian Carter advances against Williams's proposal. According to Carter,

> [t]he property identified by Williams – consciousness of one's own place in the world and of one's own activities, intentions, and purposes – may indeed constitute a plausible basis of respect of a certain kind, but there are reasons for doubting that it will constitute a basis for *equal* respect (of that kind) . . . [A]s an empirical property, it appears . . . to be possessed in different degrees by different individuals. People are more or less conscious, and more or less able to be conscious, of their own activities, their own future, of their own life plan, of the world around them, and the options it makes available to them.[13]

This objection clearly succeeds against arguments which seek to ground our moral equality in either the contents of our beliefs, aims, and plans or the abilities on which we draw when we arrive at them. As Carter correctly asserts, some people are far more aware, both of what is going on in their minds and of the options with which the world presents them, than others, and such differences are often due to deeper differences in intelligence, imagination, or other innate abilities. For this reason, neither people's beliefs, aims, and plans nor the abilities that account for these are distributed uniformly enough among persons to be the basis for their moral equality.

---

[12] *Ibid.*, p. 95.   [13] Carter, "Respect and the Basis of Equality," 547.

But this is neither the only nor the most plausible form that Williams's proposal can take. A very different version, which Carter's objection does *not* defeat, is one that focuses not on the particulars of people's beliefs, aims, or plans, but rather on the fact that each person is equally a subject *with* such mental contents. If the reason we are moral equals is simply that each of us has (is?) a subjectivity of a certain sort — that each occupies a point of view from which the world appears a certain way, certain things appear to matter, and certain courses of action appear to be open — then any variations in the contents of our beliefs and aims, and in the capacities that gave rise to these, will simply drop out as irrelevant. The thought behind this proposal is often expressed as the claim that each person is a world unto himself.

The idea that our moral equality is somehow rooted in the fact that each of us is a separate consciousness is hardly new. The phrase "each person is a world" yields over twelve million google hits, and many of these have at least vaguely egalitarian overtones (though many others instead stress human diversity in its various aspects: paths to self-fulfillment, styles of football, preferences about sexual positions, and so on). Moreover, the pervasive appeal of the impulse to link our moral equality to our subjectivity is no accident; for the subjective aspect of our consciousness is, in a number of respects, exactly the right *sort* of fact to serve as the basis for our moral equality.

For, first, because each person's subjectivity is accessible to him alone, there is a sense in which it is not an empirical fact at all. Although others can of course investigate both the physical underpinnings of what goes on in a person's mind and the behavior to which those goings-on give rise, all such investigations must be conducted from a third-personal perspective, and so cannot shed light on what things are like *for the agent himself*. Philosophers disagree about how best to accommodate this fact within a naturalistic picture of the world — this is the so-called "hard problem of consciousness"[14] — but,

---

[14] This formulation was introduced by David Chalmers; see, for example, David Chalmers, *The Conscious Mind: In Search of a Fundamental Theory* (Oxford University Press, 1996).

as Thomas Nagel has repeatedly insisted, the one response that does *not* seem acceptable is to deny that the phenomenon of subjectivity exists.[15] And because each person has a subjectivity that cannot be investigated empirically, the claim that I am advancing – that we are moral equals because we are all equally centers of consciousness – is in principle invulnerable to refutation through appeals to empirically discoverable differences.

But, second, even though the subjective aspect of our consciousness is not an *empirical* fact, it remains a fact that is capable of grounding our moral equality. Although the notion of moral equality can itself be spelled out in more than one way, the core idea is pretty clearly that each person's fundamental interests are to count equally in determining the content of the principles which in turn provide us with moral reasons for acting. In saying this, I do not mean to suggest that we never have reason to discount any actual person's interests – we certainly may discount the criminal's interest in not being punished – but I do mean that any principle that licenses this discounting must itself be established through a line of thought that attaches full weight to the would-be criminal's interests.[16] To qualify as a suitable basis for this form of equality, a class of facts need not be empirical, but its members do need to be (a) non-normative features of persons which (b) are capable of giving rise to interests which count equally in the specified sense. Although normative considerations clearly play an important role in what goes on within each person's subjectivity, the fact that they play this role is not itself normative. Thus, the facts about human subjectivity do appear to satisfy (a). The question of whether they satisfy (b) may look harder, since the mere claim that someone is a center of consciousness seems too undifferentiated to support any conclusions about his basic interests. However, I believe, and will now argue, that it is indeed possible to draw conclusions about those interests from certain structural features which are common to the subjectivities of all normal humans.

[15] Nagel has defended this view in many places; for a definitive statement, see Thomas Nagel, *The View from Nowhere* (Oxford University Press, 1986).
[16] Think, for example, of the ways in which contractualists or proponents of the impartial spectator view would approach the problem of punishment.

III

Although the structure of human consciousness has been explored in great depth by philosophers from Kant through the phenomenological movement, the features that are relevant to our current problem lie much closer to the surface. Indeed, for our purposes, what matters is simply the near-platitude that each normal person's consciousness is organized around certain fundamental assumptions. These include, but are far from exhausted by, the assumptions that the world is temporally as well as spatially ordered, that the person himself is an embodied subject who has existed in the past and will exist for at least some time in the future, that various courses of action are open to him, that the world gives him reason to do some things and refrain from doing others, and that he is, within limits, capable both of finding out what reasons he has and of acting on them. Despite the endless variety of people's thoughts, ambitions, and capacities, each has a unifying consciousness with this same generic structure.

Moreover, from the content of these organizing assumptions, we can infer that each person necessarily projects himself into the future as the continuing subject of a certain kind of life.[17] He projects himself not merely as the locus of a kaleidoscopic sequence of unrelated feelings and experiences, nor yet as a rudimentary agent who at each moment will respond to his strongest urges, but rather as a continuing conscious subject whose earlier and later experiences will be related by anticipation and memory, and whose earlier and later actions will be structured around plans that are aimed at implementing his stable though evolving reason-based aims. Of course, these projections would have little bearing on a person's moral standing if they were mistaken; but because the assumptions that give rise to the projections are built into a person's consciousness at each moment, and so will themselves persist if his consciousness does, his projections will *not* be mistaken as long as he continues to exist as the kind of conscious subject

---

[17] For elaboration of a view of this general sort, see Christine Korsgaard, "Personal Identity and the Unity of Agency: A Kantian Response to Parfit," in Christine Korsgaard, *Creating the Kingdom of Ends* (Cambridge University Press, 1996), pp. 363–97.

that he now is. Thus, in addition to dictating the synchronic structure of each person's subjectivity, the assumptions have the diachronic effect of enabling each person *to live a characteristically human life.*

These features of our consciousness provide the needed bridge between our subjectivity and our interests. If the structure of an individual's consciousness channels him into a life of a certain sort, then it must also give rise to whatever interests a life of that sort involves. Thus, because the subjectivity of each normal human makes it both possible and necessary for him to live a life that is organized around evolving sets of reason-based aims, that subjectivity must also cause each normal human to have interests that are suitably related *to* his aims. It must, for example, cause each of us to have an interest in (1) remaining alive long enough to realize various aims, (2) being free to form, revise, and pursue his intentions in accordance with (what he views as) his strongest reasons, (3) having the various things (health, resources, security, the cooperation of others) that he needs to pursue his plans successfully, and (4) actually being successful in accomplishing his aims. Although philosophers disagree about which of our shared interests are the ones in whose equal importance our moral equality resides, few would deny that the relevant interests consist either of some subset of those I have just cited or of others which are intimately related to them. By thus linking the features that structure the consciousness of each normal human being to the interests of whose equal importance our moral equality consists, we can decisively block the objection that our subjectivity is too undifferentiated to sustain the claim that we are moral equals.

IV

As we have seen, the standard attempts to reconstruct the factual basis of our moral equality fall in two main groups. One is the family of views that seek to ground our equal moral standing exclusively in the fact that each of us possesses some scalar property to a degree that surpasses some threshold or falls within some range: these are the threshold and range property views. The other is Singer's considered view, which concedes that our moral equality has a factual basis, but contends that this has nothing to do with the content or sophistication of our mental lives but instead consists simply of our sentience.[18] Against this background, my own view emerges as a kind of hybrid; for like the threshold and range property views, it appeals to certain empirical features that all normal humans share to varying degrees, but, unlike them, it invokes these features to explain only why we all *have* the interests of whose equal importance our moral equality consists. To explain why each person's interests *are* equally important, I invoke a very different sort of fact – namely, that each of us occupies a distinct subjectivity – which is at least closely related to Singer's criterion of sentience.

By thus dividing the explanatory labor, my account preserves each competitor's advantages without being saddled with its defects. To see this, consider first the threshold and range property views. Earlier on, I criticized these views on the grounds that no one has offered a convincing explanation of why, if a person's moral standing depends on his having a given empirical property, two people with very different amounts of that property can have the *same* moral standing as long as each surpasses some threshold. But if we take the structural features of our consciousness to explain only why we *have* the interests whose satisfaction matters equally, but not why their satisfaction *does* matter equally, then this problem disappears; for even if the features of our consciousness that make our characteristic interests possible do come in degrees, the interests *that* those features make possible, and their importance to their possessors, need not and do not. To have an interest in (say) accomplishing his rational ends, or in having the opportunities or resources to do so, a person need only have the sort of consciousness that enables him to *have* rational ends; and to have such a consciousness, he need only exceed some threshold of ability to think in temporal terms, assess the considerations that tell for and against different courses of action, form and execute plans on this basis, and so on. As long as two people both meet this requirement,

---

[18] For discussion that seeks to explain why views about moral standing divide along these lines, see Justin Sytsma and Edouard Machery, "The Two Sources of Moral Standing," *Review of Philosophy and Psychology* 3 (2012): 303–24.

the fact that their plans differ in complexity and sophistication will not mean that one has more of an interest in succeeding than the other. Although there are obvious questions about where to set the relevant thresholds and what to say about those who fail to come up to them, we may safely assume that all normal and near-normal humans *do* come up to them. And, because they do, the fact that they differ greatly along the relevant dimensions will not affect our ability to invoke the shared features of their consciousness to explain why they all have the sorts of interests of whose equal importance their moral equality consists.

Where the contrast with Singer's view is concerned, it is less obvious that my own proposal is an improvement; for when I attribute the equal importance of each person's interests to the fact that each is a distinct subjectivity, I am saying something that sounds a lot like what Singer says about sentience. However, when we look more closely, we find that Singer's claim and mine are not at all the same; for what he says about sentience leads directly to a question to which what I say about subjectivity provides the natural answer.

For according to Singer, the fact that people and cows but not rocks are sentient enters not to explain why the interests of all people (and, in his view, all cows) count equally, but only to explain why people and cows, but not rocks, *have* interests. Being sentient, he suggests, is important simply because it is a prerequisite for having any interests at all. By contrast, to explain why the interests of all sentient beings must be given equal consideration, he makes no further appeal to the fact of their sentience, but instead relies on the distinct normative requirement that we "give equal weight in our moral deliberations to the like interests of all those affected by our actions."[19] This principle of equal consideration of interests, he suggests, is accepted by virtually all contemporary moral theorists, and is a constitutive element of morality itself.

But even if Singer is right to view this principle as the core of our common morality — and on this point, the persistent differences in

---

[19] Peter Singer, *Practical Ethics, Third Edition* (Cambridge University Press, 2011), p. 20.

most people's attitudes toward the interests of animals and humans should give us pause – there is still a question about its basis. Exactly what is it about interests or their bearers that *warrants* their equal consideration? When philosophers ask about the factual basis of our moral equality, it is precisely this question that they are trying to answer. And because Singer does not even acknowledge the question, much less try to answer it, his account is badly incomplete.

But here again, my division of explanatory labor enables us to make progress; for unlike Singer, I do invoke a sentience-related fact to explain why each person's interests matter. This fact is, of course, precisely that of our subjectivity or interiority – that is, precisely the fact that each has a private reality which is accessible to him alone, which for him is suffused with meaning and value, and which, when it disappears, will entirely extinguish his world. There are, to be sure, many unanswered questions about *how* a person's subjectivity can confer importance on the satisfaction of the interests to which it gives rise, but there can be little doubt that it plays this role in our moral thought. As evidence, if any is needed, we may cite the persistent association of empathy – that is, the ability to imagine the reality of another – with the moral outlook. When we want to convince someone that he ought to take another's interests seriously, the standard (and often effective) way of doing so is to get him to look at the situation through the other person's eyes.

Because being sentient necessarily *involves* having a subjective perspective, the germ of the idea that each person's interests matter because he has such a perspective may already be present in Singer's view. However, because Singer expresses his view exclusively in terms such as sentience or consciousness, both of which arguably admit of degrees, his formulations obscure the crucial fact that *having a subjectivity is an all-or-nothing matter*. A person who is semi-conscious, or who is fully awake but intellectually primitive or very stupid, has no less complete a subjectivity than a hyper-alert sophisticate. This all-or-nothing aspect of our subjectivity is crucial to my argument because it implies that the moral standing to which the subjectivities of different individuals give rise is all-or-nothing as well. If each of us is equally the occupant of a perspective of the relevant sort, and if it is simply a person's occupying such a perspective that confers importance on the satisfaction of his interests, then the interests of all persons must count the same. Thus, by grounding each person's moral standing in the subjective aspect of his consciousness, we can explain not only why each person's interests matter, but also why the satisfaction of each person's interests matters equally.

This explanation is not intended to convince the moral skeptic. There is, as far as I can see, no way of satisfying someone who does not see why we should acknowledge any moral requirements at all, or why any facts should ever support any normative conclusions. However, because we are already operating within the framework of political (and personal) morality – because it is agreed on all sides that individuals and governments *are* subject to moral demands, and that the interests of (at least) every normal human being *do* count equally in the reasoning that gives rise to moral principles – the problem I need to solve is considerably less daunting. Instead of having to explain how any facts can possibly give rise to any normative requirements, I need only explain why facts that I have singled out are the best candidates to fill a theoretical role whose contours are dictated by the normative beliefs that we already hold. That much I hope I have indeed accomplished.

V

This is a book about distributive justice, and my aim in discussing the factual basis of our moral equality has been only to find out what it can tell us about the proper distribution of goods among normal humans. Thus, with my account of that factual basis in place, I am now in a position to resume the book's main thread. However, before I do, I want to pause briefly to acknowledge a question that is not strictly relevant to my argument, but is sure to have occurred to many readers: namely, what does my account imply about the moral standing of beings *other* than normal humans?

The central issue here is easily stated. I have argued that the reason each normal human's interests are equally important is that each normal human has a distinct subjectivity. However, as far as we can tell, the members of many other species — certainly apes, cows, and voles, perhaps also grackles, carp, and lobsters — also have distinct subjectivities. Thus, doesn't my explanatory hypothesis commit me to endorsing Singer's view that the interests of each such creature are as important as those of any normal human being?

This question is harder than it looks, and any attempt to answer it would take us far afield. For this reason, I will here restrict myself to bringing out a few of the complications that make a quick answer impossible. Of these complications, one set arises when we ask exactly what it means to say that animals and humans are moral equals while another is raised by an ambiguity in my explanatory hypothesis.

Consider first the content of the claim that animals and humans have equal moral standing. I suggested above that what we mean when we say that all normal *humans* are moral equals is that each person's fundamental aim-related interests — I have not yet specified which these are — should count equally in our moral calculations. However, few if any non-human animals have subjectivities that involve a sense of themselves as persisting through time or an awareness of reasons, and so few if any have fundamental interests of the relevant kind. This raises the question about how we can best extend our claim that all normal humans are moral equals so that it applies to all such animals as well.

There are, I think, two main possibilities, the first of which is to follow Singer in taking the claim that animals and humans are moral equals to assert only that the *like* interests of the members of each species should count equally in our moral calculations. Under this interpretation, the claim that humans and animals are moral equals will assert only that

(1)   When an animal and a human both have an interest in having X, each being's interest should count equally in our moral calculations.

As so interpreted, the claim will apply only to whatever narrow range of interests humans share with animals. Especially if we focus on the shared interest that is most often cited — namely, the interest in avoiding suffering — this version of the claim has considerable appeal.

However, despite Singer's endorsement, this interpretation is neither the only nor the most natural one. In its place, we might say, with at least as much justice, that what the moral equality of animals and humans comes to is that the interests of each *which are of comparable urgency or importance for their possessors* should count equally. Under this interpretation, the claim that humans and animals are moral equals will assert that

(2)   When a human has an interest in having X and an animal an interest in having Y, the animal's interest should count as much as the human's if each occupies the same rank, on some relevant scale, relative to its bearer's other interests.

Because this version of the moral equality claim implies that the most important interest of each field mouse or prairie dog – whatever interest that might be – must count as much in our moral calculations as the most important interest of any human being, it is far less appealing than its more modest cousin.[20]

The second complication that I want to examine concerns my claim that it is the subjectivity of normal humans that accounts for their moral equality, and the question here is how much should be packed into that claim's explanatory hypothesis. Because the subjectivity of each normal human has the same structural features, and because each such subjectivity therefore gives rise to the same sorts of aim-related interests, I have so far had no occasion to ask whether what is doing the explanatory work is simply the fact that each of us *has* a subjectivity or, more elaborately, that each has a subjectivity with just the relevant features. Under the first interpretation, my explanatory hypothesis will assert that

(3)   normal human beings are moral equals simply because each has a distinct subjectivity.

---

[20]   Although Singer generally restricts himself to (1), he seems to rely on something like (2) when he writes that "In considering the ethics of the use of animal products for human food in industrial societies, we are considering a situation in which a relatively minor human interest must be balanced against the lives and welfare of the animals involved. The principle of equal consideration of interests does not allow major interests to be sacrificed for minor interests" (*ibid.*, p. 54).

Under the second, it will assert that

(4) normal human beings are moral equals because each has a distinct
     subjectivity *with the kind of structure that gives rise to a sense of
     time, reasons-responsiveness, and the interests that rational aims
     generate.*

Because the members of many animal species do have distinct subjectivities, the first hypothesis (claim (3)) may indeed support the
conclusion that many animals are the moral equals of normal humans
(although what this comes to will of course depend on how we resolve
the first of our complications). However, because few if any animals
have subjectivities of the kind that gives rise to rational aims or the
associated interests, the second hypothesis (claim (4)) will at best
imply that very few animals are the moral equals of normal humans,
and will probably not imply that any are.[21]

Because the two complications cut across each other, the question
of what my argument implies about the moral status of animals has a
wide range of (epistemically) possible answers. If we accept claims (3)
and (2), and maintain that all centers of subjectivity are of equal moral
importance and that the equally ranked interests of each therefore
have the same weight, then we will take animals and humans to be
moral equals in a very strong sense. If we accept claims (3) and (1), and
maintain that all centers of subjectivity are of equal moral importance
but that only the interests that moral equals have in common have the
same weight, then we will still take animals and humans to be moral
equals, but will do so in a much weaker sense. If we accept claim (4),

---

[21] Is (4) consistent with my claim to have divided the explanatory labor by invoking
      the features that structure our consciousness to explain why we have the interests
      we do and the distinctness of our subjective perspectives to explain why those
      interests matter equally for each person? Because (4) incorporates the features that
      structure each person's consciousness into its description of the subjectivities whose
      distinctness is said to explain why each person's relevant aim-related interests matter
      equally, there is a sense in which the answer to this question is "no." However, even
      if we accept (4), we will still be able to say that it is the shared structural features
      of our consciousness that explain why we all have the same sorts of aim-related
      interests, but that it is the separateness of our (temporally organized and reason-
      oriented) subjective perspectives that explains why the satisfaction of the relevant
      interests is equally important for each person. Because it will remain possible to say
      this, the basic division-of-labor idea will be preserved.

and maintain that humans owe their moral equality to the fact that each has a subjectivity with certain structural elements, then the fact that animals lack such subjectivities will mean that they are *not* our moral equals, and so the choice between (1)'s constricted and (2)'s expansive answer to the question of which of the interests of moral equals must count equally will not matter.

Just for the record, my own inclination is to combine (2) with a qualified version of (4). Although I accept (4)'s claim that humans owe their moral equality to the fact that each has a subjectivity with the relevant structural features, I also think that even subjectivities that lack these features confer some moral significance on their bearers. I am therefore attracted to the view that the kinds of subjectivities that animals have confer on the interests that occupy each rank for each animal an importance that is similar in kind, but lesser in weight, than the correspondingly ranked interest of a human being (or of another animal with a more complex form of subjectivity). However, to back this (or any other) answer with an argument, I would indeed have to rely on some sort of metaphysical account that goes far beyond anything I have said. Thus, having identified what I take to be the main questions that the moral standing of animals (and, *mutatis mutandis*, of drastically impaired humans) raises about my argument, I will simply leave the matter here.

CHAPTER 6

Completing the turn

In the previous chapter, I proposed an account of what it is about us that makes us moral equals. Now, with that account in hand, I want to return to the distributive questions that are my main concern. In the current chapter, I will argue, first, that the same considerations that account for our moral equality also tell for the equal distribution of a certain (rather abstract) good among us, and, second, that achieving this form of distributive equality means accepting many of the inequalities that stem from differences in the parties' choices. By integrating equality and choice in this way, we will both complete the monistic turn that Dworkin's discussion began and put ourselves in a position to resolve many further distributive questions.

I

It is widely believed that the ultimate justification for any set of social arrangements is that they advance the interests of those who live under them. This is of course only a necessary condition, since even a universally beneficial set of arrangements will not be justified if it distributes the relevant benefits and burdens sufficiently unfairly (or, perhaps, if its rationale is not in some sense available or acceptable to all affected parties); but it is widely viewed as true as far as it goes. Although the condition's acceptance may not be quite universal – some organicists may believe, instead, that societies or states have independent moral standing, and that their interests have more weight than those of some or even all combinations of individuals – I will, in what follows, simply assume that it is correct. I will assume, as well, that although each state's institutions affect many who live beyond its borders, the persons whose interests are primarily relevant to their justification include only those who do or will fall under its dominion.

Bearing these assumptions in mind, let us turn to the question of how the benefits that flow from a society's institutional arrangements should be distributed. This question derives its urgency from the fact that each person's life-prospects are profoundly affected by the legal, political, and economic institutions under which he lives. Although the person's actions will of course play a crucial role in determining his fate, it is the social background that determines what range of actions is available to him, what sorts of resources he can draw on when acting, and what the outcomes of the available actions are likely to be. Because the effects of a society's arrangements are so pervasive, the question of how its institutions should distribute resources, opportunities, and other goods is clearly a pressing one.

Our initial assumptions can take us some distance toward an answer. If a society's institutions exist only to benefit individuals, and if the relevant individuals include only those whose lives will be ordered by the institutions, then it is just the impact of the institutions on these individuals that we must consider. Moreover, because those individuals are moral equals, it seems safe to assume that the institutions must be configured in ways that benefit them all, and that they must do so in a way that accords the interests of each the same weight. By thus narrowing the field of defensible institutions, we can delineate the space within which an adequate distributive theory is to be found.

But although this narrowing is clearly helpful, it leaves the two main substantive questions unresolved. Of these questions, the first is which goods are of primary distributive concern. This question is important both because there are a number of live candidates – welfare, resources, primary goods, opportunities, and capabilities are among the most prominent – and because distributing any one of these goods in accordance with a given pattern is likely to cause the others to be distributed very differently. The second unresolved question is how the preferred good (and thus, derivatively, each of the others) is to *be* distributed. The answer cannot be simply that the best distribution is one that takes account of the interests of every citizen; for many distributive patterns can be said to do this, each in its own way. We may, for example, be said to take equal account of the interests of all citizens by distributing the relevant good equally among them, by adopting some equality-related approach such as priority, sufficiency, or the difference principle, by pursuing some form of maximizing consequentialism, or even by allowing the good's distribution to be determined by some kind of fair competition. To decide among these possibilities, we will have to supplement our assumptions about the aims of government and the moral equality of persons with an appeal to some relevant substantive consideration.

II

And this is where the factual basis of our moral equality comes in. Because the sense in which we are moral equals is that our interests are of equal importance, there is bound to be some sort of internal connection between the facts about us in virtue of which we are moral equals and the nature of the interests of whose equal importance our moral equality consists. The nature of those interests, in its turn, is bound to have implications about how different goods are related to them. In the previous chapter, I argued that the reason we are moral equals is that each of us is a distinct subjectivity whose consciousness is structured by a set of very general beliefs – the same ones in each case – that make it both possible and necessary for him to live a characteristic human life. Although people of course vary greatly in many dimensions, the common structure of their consciousness channels each into a life that is future-oriented, active, reason-guided, and organized around an enduring though evolving set of aims. Taking my cue from this, I now want to suggest that each person's most fundamental interest consists precisely of living the sort of life that his form of mental organization makes possible.

Because this suggestion is bound to be controversial, I must say something in its defense. The controversy, I expect, will center not on the claim that each person *has* an interest in living the life that lies before him – who could deny this? – but rather on its being each person's most *fundamental* interest. The obvious objection is that each of us has a large and disorderly set of further interests, many of which involve the achievement of the various goals that we view as worth seeking and many others of which involve the acquisition of various prerequisites for successful goal-seeking, and that these tend to dominate our thinking. Because it is our specific projects that occupy our attention and energy, it is tempting to view the interests associated with (some of) them as fundamental.

However, to frame the issue in this way is to create an opposition where none really exists. Because our projects are all embedded in our larger lives, the interests to which they give rise are simply *components* of our interest in living as we see fit. Moreover, because all of our projects are subject to revision, the interests to which they give rise cannot be as fundamental as our interest in exercising the judgmental capacities on which their continued existence depends. Although it has become popular to speak of "ground projects" that are so important to us that they give us "reason to go on,"[1] and of "practical identities" that provide us with our most fundamental (non-moral) reasons,[2] our stubborn endurance in the face of the utter collapse of our projects suggests that these claims contain a healthy measure of hyperbole. From our standpoint as practical agents confronting (what we must regard as) our partially open future, our most fundamental interest must lie precisely in navigating the vicissitudes of that future.

Taking this claim as our starting point, let us now ask what follows both about which goods best serve our fundamental interest and about how our institutions should distribute those goods. At first glance, the answer in each case may appear to be "very little"; for if what makes us moral equals is the fact that each has a life of his own to live, then nothing short of death will frustrate the interest that is singled out by that fact. Because each person will live his life in any case, his doing so will be affected by neither his absolute nor his relative amounts

[1] Bernard Williams, "Persons, Character, and Morality," in his *Moral Luck* (Cambridge University Press, 1981), pp. 1–19.
[2] See Christine M. Korsgaard, *The Sources of Normativity* (Cambridge University Press, 1996), and *Self-Constitution: Agency, Identity, and Integrity* (Oxford University Press, 2009).

of welfare, resources, or opportunities. And, for this reason, the facts that underlie our moral standing may appear to have no bearing on either the priority relations among these goods or the principles that ought to guide their distribution.

But this objection proceeds too quickly; for from the claim that each person has a fundamental interest in living his own life, and thus in performing the activities of which living a characteristically human life consists, it simply does not follow that anyone who remains alive and intact will automatically realize that interest. The reason this does not follow is that the relevant activities – assessing the reasons with which one's evolving situation provides one, forming and pursuing aims, intentions, and plans that reflect those assessments, and so on – all have standards of success built right into them. This is true not only of practical and theoretical reasoning, which obviously can be done well or badly, but also of purposive activity; for anyone who entertains a purpose is thereby submitting himself to a standard that favors its achievement. Because we can always fall short of meeting the standards implicit in these activities, and because our fundamental interest is not merely in engaging in the activities but in doing so successfully, merely living a long time does not guarantee the realization of one's fundamental interest. And, because of this, there is ample room for the question of which social arrangements are most conducive to that interest's general satisfaction.

There is obviously much more to say about the fundamental interest to which the facts that ground our moral standing give rise, and I will try to say some of it in the next chapter. However, for now, what matters is simply that that interest is bound to extend far beyond the mere performance of the generic activities into which the structure of our consciousness channels us. As a placeholder for whichever further elements are involved, I will say that each of us has a fundamental interest in living his life *effectively*.

III

Even without further elaboration, we can see that there are many ways in which a person can fail to live his life effectively. He can fail to do so because he is too malnourished to think clearly, because he is too poor to have any meaningful options, because his environment is too chaotic or unstable to enable him to plan, because he is under the sway of another's will, or for any number of other reasons. Of these causes of failure, many are rooted in adverse socio-economic conditions, and many of these adverse conditions are remediable. Thus, the obvious way to make progress in deciding how a society should distribute various goods among its members is to ask which distributive arrangements are most consistent with an equal weighting of its members' fundamental interest in living their lives effectively.

That will depend, of course, on what effectively living one's life involves. Because that notion has not yet been discussed in detail, it may seem necessary to defer this part of our discussion until we have clarified it. But that is not the strategy that I will adopt; for, as will become clear, we can advance a surprising distance toward a substantive distributive theory without saying anything more about what living one's life effectively involves.

Let us take as our point of departure the familiar debate about whether societies should focus their distributive efforts on resources, opportunities, welfare, capabilities, primary goods, or something else. Although this debate has been conducted at an exceptionally high philosophical level, it has not resulted in much narrowing of the options: the competing positions are, if anything, even more entrenched now than they were when the debate began. The reason for the standoff, as I see it, is that although all the participants in the debate would agree that persons are moral equals,[3] and although each would presumably want his account of which goods matter most to reflect this fact, none has tried to specify what it is about us that *makes* us moral equals. This lack of specificity means that none is in a position to appeal to any aspect of our nature to explain *why* the particular good he favors matters most. In contrast, by grounding the moral equality of persons in the fact that each is a separate

---

[3] For an argument that there is consensus on this point, see Amartya Sen, *Inequality Reexamined* (Oxford University Press, 1992), chapter 1.

consciousness of a sort that gives rise to a specific fundamental interest, we gain a touchstone against which to test the different claims about which goods it is most important to distribute properly. For if our characteristic form of consciousness gives each of us a fundamental interest in living his life effectively, then the relative importance of the different goods whose distribution is in question must be a function of their relative ability to *advance* that fundamental interest.

It is clearly important to be able to impose an ordering on questions about how to distribute resources, welfare, opportunities, and the rest. However, an even more important implication of what has been said is that there is a further good whose distribution is more important than that of *any* of these entries. For if we take the ways in which resources, opportunities, and the rest should be distributed to depend on their contributions to people's abilities to live their lives effectively, then we will in effect be treating the ability to live one's life effectively as a good in its own right – one that is more abstract than the goods with whose distribution philosophers have usually been concerned, but one which is, for that very reason, more basic. We will be saying, as well, that the primary distributive question, on whose answer the others all turn, is how the good of being able to live one's life effectively should itself be distributed among a society's members by its basic institutions.

The idea that a society's institutions must enable its members to determine the course of their own lives is of course not new. It is closely linked to the familiar principle that government must not promote any particular conception of the good, but must simply provide a neutral and just framework within which each citizen can pursue the good as he understands it.[4] I think, and have argued at length, that this principle is indefensible;[5] but I also think that

---

[4] For important statements of this view, see John Rawls, *A Theory of Justice* (Cambridge, MA: Harvard University Press, 1971); Robert Nozick, *Anarchy, State, and Utopia* (New York: Basic Books, 1974); Bruce Ackerman, *Social Justice and the Liberal State* (New Haven: Yale University Press, 1980); Ronald Dworkin, *A Matter of Principle* (Cambridge, MA: Harvard University Press, 1985); and Charles Larmore, *Patterns of Moral Complexity* (Cambridge University Press, 1987).

[5] George Sher, *Beyond Neutrality: Perfectionism and Politics* (Cambridge University Press, 1997).

by reconceiving as goods the activities it seeks to protect, we will fundamentally transform our current inquiry. More specifically, by taking as basic the question of how society should distribute the abstract good of being able to live one's life effectively, we will come to see both how the moral equality of persons can justify a particular egalitarian principle of distribution and how that principle can in turn justify various important inequalities. In this way, we will come to see what is true and important about Dworkin's attempt to establish an internal connection between distributive equality and choice-related inequality.

IV

There is, notoriously, a gap between the claim that each member of a society has an interest in having a certain good and the claim that the society must provide each member with an equal amount *of* that good. This is the gap that utilitarians and libertarians both exploit when they reject the inference from the premise that each of us has an interest in being happy or rich to the conclusion that our social institutions should distribute happiness and/or wealth equally among us. It is important to note, moreover, that this gap does not disappear when we factor in our earlier assumptions that each society's institutions exist only for its members' benefit and that those members are moral equals. Even if everyone would benefit from being happy or rich, and even if social institutions exist precisely to benefit those who live under them, there will still be a question about why the right *way* for a society to benefit its members is to provide them with either of these goods. Moreover, even if this *is* the right way for a society to benefit its members, there will remain a further question about why their moral equality should require that each be provided with the same *amount* of happiness or wealth.

The challenge I must meet to establish that societies must provide their members with equal amounts of the abstract good of being able to live their lives effectively, therefore, is to explain how what is unique about that good can help us to answer these questions. As a first step toward meeting this challenge, let us return to our observation that the facts in which the moral equality of persons is grounded imply that each person's deepest *interest* is in living his own life effectively. This observation is significant because the obvious way to make sense of the idea that a society's institutions must benefit those who live under them is precisely to tie the relevant form of benefit to whichever of the parties' interests is most fundamental. That is what Rawls does when he argues that his theory of justice is appropriate to a society of persons whose highest-order interests are to realize and exercise their two moral powers – namely, "to understand, to apply and to act from (and not merely in accordance with) the principles of justice" and "to form, to revise, and rationally to pursue a conception of the good"[6] – and although my account of our fundamental interest is both less moralized and more oriented to our factual nature than Rawls's, it is what I want to do as well. If I am right in maintaining that each person's deepest interest is in living his own life effectively, then the obvious way for a society to benefit its members will indeed be by advancing that interest.

This implication, moreover, provides a convincing answer to the question of why the right way for a society to advance its members' interests is to provide them with a certain type of *good*. That question gets much of its bite from our resistance to the obnoxious idea of government as a kind of benevolent paterfamilias whose role is to bestow gifts of happiness or wealth on its dependent citizens/children. It also draws force from certain more focused objections: many (myself included) find it bizarre to take the state's distributive aims to include brightening the lives of the gloomy or compensating those with unchosen expensive tastes, while many others (myself not included) hold that governments lack the standing to redistribute wealth or resources because doing so violates people's natural property rights. But whatever force these objections have against the view that a society's institutional arrangements must provide its members with the goods of welfare or resources, they have none against the view that those arrangements must enable the society's members to live their own

---

[6] John Rawls, "Kantian Constructivism in Moral Theory: The Dewey Lectures 1980," *Journal of Philosophy* 77 (1980): 515–72, at 525.

lives effectively. The objections lack force against this view because it does not portray individuals as passive recipients of the state's largesse; does not overemphasize the importance of their satisfactions and affective states; and can simply incorporate whatever constraints a preinstitutional set of property rights might be thought to impose. And, hence, because there is no real difference between making it possible for someone to live his life effectively and providing him with the good of being able to do so, the objections also lack force against the idea that a society's arrangements should seek to provide its members with that abstract good.

It is, however, not yet clear why a society must seek to provide each of its members with an equal *amount* of that abstract good. Although this obviously has something to do with the fact that all persons are moral equals, what needs to be explained is how we can get from moral to distributive equality. This question would not arise if the ability to live one's life effectively were an all-or-nothing matter; for in that case providing each member of a society with some amount of that good would be *equivalent* to providing each with an equal amount. However, even in the absence of a detailed account, it is clear that the good is not all-or-nothing; for agents can be more or less adept at practical and theoretical reasoning, be more or less ingenious at achieving their aims, have more or less access to resources and opportunities, and so on. Thus, to complete the transition from my account of the basis of people's moral equality to the relevant abstract egalitarian principle, I will indeed have to address the further question.

As a first step toward an answer, we must remind ourselves that although a society's obligation to enable its members to live their lives effectively applies to them one by one, the content of that obligation is the same in every case. Because the society's members are moral equals, and because each has a fundamental interest in living his life effectively, any reason that the society has to create the conditions under which one of them can live his life with a particular degree of effectiveness must be matched by a reason of similar strength for each other member. When this collection of individual reasons is considered in the aggregate, it adds up to a single omnibus reason to elevate all citizens above some threshold of effectiveness. Although this omnibus reason piggybacks on the narrower reasons that it aggregates, the situation for which it tells – bringing everyone above the relevant threshold – remains distinct from the one for which any of them tells.

Although this reasoning calls for a form of equal treatment, its requirements will not be violated if some citizens merely reach the threshold while others surpass it. Thus, if my argument ended here, it would support a version of sufficientarianism rather than egalitarianism. This would not be a bad result, and I would be happy to accept it as a fall-back position. However, I don't think I need to accept it; for we can move past sufficiency to equality by showing that the ability to live one's life effectively belongs to the class of hybrid goods which only remain a matter of degree until the factors that contribute to their existence reach a certain level, but which become all-or-nothing afterwards. There are, in fact, many such goods. For example, although a person who must subsist on 800 calories a day is less well nourished than one who consumes 1,200, a person who consumes 2,500 calories a day is no less well nourished than one who consumes 3,000.[7] Once the crucial threshold is reached, no further increment in the number of calories consumed can increase a person's level of nourishment. And although I won't be able to argue the point until we have looked more carefully at the notion of effectiveness, I believe something similar holds for the ability to live effectively: that once a person attains a certain level of wealth, opportunity, knowledge, and skill, his ability to compensate for his remaining limitations is such that no further increment in any of these dimensions will bring a further increase in his ability to live effectively.

If I am right about this, and if the threshold of effectiveness to which the state is obligated to elevate a person coincides with the level at which no further increases are possible, then there will indeed be

---

[7] Compare Joseph Raz: "Satiable principles are marked by one feature: the demands the principles impose can be completely met. When they are completely met then whatever may happen and whatever might have happened the principles cannot be, nor could they have been, satisfied to a higher degree" (Raz, *The Morality of Freedom* (Oxford University Press, 1986), pp. 235–36.

a sense in which my account is egalitarian as well as sufficientarian. If the upper limit of effectiveness is the same for each person, then the account will be egalitarian in the strong sense of implying that there can be no just situation in which any person either exceeds or falls below a single threshold of effectiveness. If instead the upper limit differs from person to person, as the analogy with nourishment suggests, then the account will be egalitarian in the weaker (but still far from trivial) sense of implying that there can be no just situation in which any person is less able to live effectively than he could possibly be. Because I don't think the upper limit can be the same for all, my final position will be egalitarian in this second, weaker sense.

V

Bearing all this in mind, let us return to what has been this book's guiding question. Why, exactly, should someone who is committed to distributive equality make an exception for inequalities that can be traced to the parties' choices? I argued in the earlier chapters that Dworkin was right to seek a unified justification of both the commitment and the exception in the deeper fact of our moral equality, but that his inattention to the grounding of our moral equality left him without resources to provide the needed justification. Now, after moving from an examination of that grounding to a new account of the good whose distribution is primarily in question, I want to revisit the issue. Can we infer, from the premise that societies are obligated to provide their members with equal (or sufficient) measures of the good of being able to live their lives effectively, that they must also accept various inequalities that reflect differences in the members' choices?

The answer, I think, is that we can; for whatever else is true, a person is definitely *not* able to live his life effectively if his fortunes are systematically disconnected from his own decisions and actions. Someone whose deliberations never ended in decisions, whose decisions never issued in actions, or whose actions never affected his life in predictable ways would hardly be living his own life at all. He would be more a patient than an agent. Thus, to equalize its members' abilities to live their lives effectively, a society must, at a minimum, maintain social arrangements that generally allow the predictable consequences of their decisions to play themselves out. It must, among other things, give each person enough latitude to shape his own destiny. However, this will inevitably lead to inequality over time for the simple reason that people are not all equally *good* at shaping their own destinies.

For as we have already seen, some are far better than others at processing information, envisioning alternatives, estimating probabilities, deferring gratification, and the like. As a result, some are bound to react to any given situation by making decisions which will render them less able than their fellows to live their lives effectively in the future. Some, like Whisper, Brooke, and Dr. Rosen, will do foolish things that drastically limit their future options; others will squander their resources and incur large debts; still others will act in ways that ruin their health. By contrast, others again will make decisions that are unusually shrewd or prudent, and so will end up better off than most. As these examples suggest, the effects of a person's actions which are capable of compromising or enhancing his future prospects are not merely economic, but also extend into the legal, physical, and social realms. Since no society can prevent its members from getting into legal trouble, acting in unhealthy ways, or rendering themselves obnoxious to others, there is no realistic possibility of eliminating such effects.

When Whisper and Brooke and Dr. Rosen make the foolish choices that compromise their future prospects, they do not fully satisfy the standards that are internal to the activities into which their consciousness channels them. A person who cannot meet those standards is not fully able to live his life effectively. Thus, it may seem possible to block my argument by pointing out that agents who make choices that leave them worse off than others are *ipso facto not* as able as those others to live their lives effectively. But, for two reasons, this objection does not succeed. One obvious problem with it is that it blurs the distinction between those who lack an ability and those who merely fail to exercise it on a particular occasion. (Dr. Rosen, for example, may well fall in the latter category.) However, the far more serious difficulty is that even if the vast majority of those who make foolish choices *are* deficient in imagination, intelligence, good judgment, or some other mental component of the ability to live one's life effectively, these deficits are often both innate and intractable. Although a supportive and stimulating environment can obviously help, there are many who from the beginning lack discernment, strength of will, or simple common sense. Where such agents are concerned, the best that their society can do, and hence the most that it can be obligated *to* do, is provide the requisite supportive environment. Thus, to sidestep the objection, we need only replace the argument's original claim – that even if a society equalizes its members' ability to live their lives effectively, the choices through which they exercise that ability will soon lead to inequalities – with the equally defensible but more widely applicable claim that even if a society *goes as far as it can in the direction* of equalizing its members' ability to live their lives effectively, the choices through which they exercise that ability will soon lead to inequalities. However, for brevity, I will for the most part ignore this complication and stick to the claim's simpler version.

When agents who are equally able to live their lives effectively exercise that ability differently, the variation in their choices can give rise to inequalities of two very different sorts. On the one hand, their different choices can obviously cause them to have different amounts of such familiar goods as welfare, resources, and opportunities. However, in addition, because adequate levels of resources and opportunities are themselves prerequisites for the ability to live one's life effectively, the choices that cause people to have unequal amounts of these goods may also cause them to become unequal *in their ability to live their lives effectively*. In this way, the ability to live one's life effectively may sometimes be self-undermining.

Because living one's life effectively at t1 means making decisions that may affect one's ability to live effectively at t2, any society that seeks to equalize its members' overall abilities to live their lives effectively must decide on which stages of their lives to concentrate its efforts. At first glance, the three main options appear to be (1) always to allow them to make, and live with the consequences of, their own decisions; (2) always to (try to) protect them from whichever consequences of their decisions will reduce their ability to live effectively in the future; or (3) to allow them to live with some, but not all, of the consequences of their decisions that will have this effect. Understood as responses to the question of when in a person's life he must have as much as possible of the good of being able to live his life effectively, the first alternative tells us always to sacrifice the later for the earlier, the second tells us always to sacrifice the earlier for the later, while the third asserts that neither the earlier nor the later should take absolute priority, but that how much of the good a person should have at any given time should be determined in some other way.

Although the issues here are complicated, I will eventually come down in favor of a version of the third alternative. However, for now, it is less important to choose between (1) and (3) than it is to see that we must reject (2). Put most simply, the reason a society cannot possibly adopt a general policy of protecting people's ability to live their lives effectively at later moments by preventing them from doing so at earlier moments is that, under such a policy, the future will never arrive. At each later moment, there will be new reasons to prevent people from living their lives effectively in order to protect their ability to do so at still later moments. Under a policy of this sort, those with chronically bad judgment will never be able to make meaningful choices, while those who are intermittently foolish or impulsive will periodically but regularly find their decisions blocked or undone. Such a policy would be self-defeating because a person whose every bad decision was blocked or prevented from taking effect could not follow through on his plans in the way that living his own life requires. In addition, it is questionable whether even a wise and prudent person can really be said to be living his own life if his good decisions are only allowed to take effect because they will *not* undermine his future ability to live effectively.[8] To avoid these

---

[8] Harry Frankfurt has convincingly argued that a person in this situation would be *responsible* for his decisions and their effects – see Frankfurt, "Alternate Possibilities and Moral Responsibility," *Journal of Philosophy* 66 (1969): 829–39 – but whether such a person would be either free or genuinely self-governing is a further question. As Philip Pettit has noted, "[o]n the currently standard analysis, agents enjoy freedom in a choice between certain options, just insofar as those are truly options for the agent" (Phillip Pettit, "Freedom and Probability: A Comment on Goodin and Jackson,"

difficulties, we must accept as legitimate many of the later inequalities that the earlier equal distribution of the good of being able to live one's life effectively makes necessary. However, to say this is just to agree that any defensible principle that calls for the equal distribution of the good of being able to live one's life effectively must contain a built-in exception for certain inequalities that can be traced to the parties' own previous choices.

VI

Like luck egalitarianism, the view that I have proposed asserts that inequalities in the distribution of the good(s) with which justice is concerned are sometimes justified by the fact that they are due to differences in the parties' choices. However, unlike luck egalitarianism, this view offers a promising explanation of *why* these inequalities are justified. It explains this not by taking justice to require only the elimination of inequalities that are due to luck rather than choice, nor yet by embracing Dworkin's claims about offsetting resources and hypothetical insurance schemes, none of which turned out to have much to do with choice, but rather by retaining the luck egalitarians' emphasis on choice while rejecting their insistence that its significance lies in its opposition to luck. Instead of stressing the definitional connection between choice and the absence of luck, the proposed account appeals to the very different analytic connection between living one's life effectively and making choices that stick. By combining this analytic connection with the claim that a just society must allow each of its members to live his life effectively, the account connects choice to justice by maintaining that making choices whose predictable consequences are allowed to play themselves out is itself an integral part of the good whose just distribution is in question.

By thus decoupling choice from (the absence of) luck and relocating its significance in its relation to the activity of living one's life effectively, we shift the axis of our discussion. Instead of having

Philosophy and Public Affairs 36 (2008): 239–65, at 211–12. Pettit cites a number of relevant works in footnote 16 of his essay.

to ask which inequalities are matters of luck and how these can be
neutralized, we now face a battery of new questions about the notion
of living one's life effectively. Of these new questions, some concern
the notion's exact content and its relation to the generic facts about
our consciousness that were seen to ground our moral equality, others concern the connections between living one's life effectively and
having such familiar goods as resources, opportunities, and welfare,
others again concern the factors that determine the thresholds that
govern both the ability to live effectively and the factors that contribute to it, and yet others concern the tradeoffs between exercising
that ability at earlier moments and retaining it at later ones. These
new questions are every bit as complex and difficult as the ones they
replace, and they will occupy us for the remainder of the book. However, before I turn to them, I want briefly to mention one respect in
which our new orientation represents not a complication but a radical
simplification.

What has been simplified is the task of achieving an adequate
understanding of choice itself. That task poses problems for those
who take justice to require the elimination of all inequalities that are
due to luck, and who locate the significance of choice exclusively in its
opposition to luck, because each person's choices are in part a function
of native abilities that he did not choose in their turn. As we have
seen, a person can only choose to perform an action if he recognizes
it as available, and can only choose to perform it on the basis of a
particular good- or right-making feature if he thinks it has that feature.
These facts are significant because imagination and discernment are
not themselves chosen, but are gifts which different people possess
to different degrees. And, more generally, it is hard to deny that
"[f]avorable or unfavorable genetic inheritance and early childhood
socialization experiences crucially affect any adult individual's ability
to make sensible choices and implement them" and that "[e]ven if we
have freedom of the will, empirical helps and hindrances to exercising
it virtuously fall randomly in different amounts on different persons."[9]

---

[9] Richard J. Arneson, "Egalitarianism and the Undeserving Poor," *Journal of Political
Philosophy* 5 (1997): 327–50, at 332.

This entanglement of choice with unchosen ability is a major complication for any egalitarian who wishes to eliminate the effects of luck. To accommodate it, he must either reject all inequalities that are due to differences in choice which in turn reflect unchosen differences in choice-making ability, or else determine *how much* of each inequality is due to such a difference and then reject just that portion of it.[10] But if what is important about choice is not that it is the complement of luck, but rather that it is integral to living one's life effectively, then no such maneuver will be needed. Because our orientation as agents is outward toward the world and forward toward the future, the question of whether our cognitive and executive abilities enable us to live effectively depends not on whether we have chosen them, but only on what they allow us to choose and do. Whatever the sources or limits of our choice-making abilities, to live our lives is simply to make our choices within the parameters they impose. Thus, if our choices confer legitimacy upon the inequalities to which they give rise in virtue of the fact that choosing is integral to living effectively, then there is no reason to believe that they can only play this role if they are entirely untainted by luck.

To say this is not to deny that living one's life effectively means exercising a certain form of control, but it *is* to deny that such control must be either deep or total or metaphysical. What someone needs to live his life effectively is not control "all the way down," but only an adequate range of options and an adequate measure of ability to recognize and respond to them. Just what the latter abilities come to, and how a society should deal with inequalities that arise because some people lack them, are questions that must await our examination of what is involved in living one's life effectively. However, even before we undertake that examination, we can see that the necessary form of control extends only to a person's actions going forward and not to the abilities that enable him to perform them.

[10] For two ways of developing the idea that society should seek to eliminate only that proportion of each inequality for which the relevant agents are not responsible, see John Roemer, "A Pragmatic Theory of Responsibility for the Egalitarian Planner," *Philosophy and Public Affairs* 22 (1993): 146–66, and Peter Vallentyne, "Brute Luck and Responsibility," *Politics, Philosophy, and Economics* 7 (2008): 57–80.

The shallowness of the requisite form of control also allows us to avoid the related but more general problem that determinism is sometimes said to pose for luck egalitarianism. Because we obviously lack control over the causal determinants of our choices – these are, for the most part, quite unknown to us – determinism implies that all of our choices, and so too all of the inequalities to which they contribute, are in one recognizable sense a matter of luck. This is sometimes taken to show that luck egalitarians can only endorse inequalities that stem from differences in choice if determinism is false. As Samuel Scheffler has put the point, "the plausibility of a luck-egalitarian position tacitly depends on a libertarian conception of what genuine choice would look like."[11] Because even many luck egalitarians who reject Scheffler's diagnosis would agree that determinism somehow needs to be dealt with, many would concur with Gerald Cohen's often-quoted assertion that "we may indeed be up to our necks in the free will problem, but that is just tough luck."[12]

But this problem, too, disappears when we detach the significance of choice from its supposed opposition to luck. If what justifies inequalities that stem from differences in choice is not that they are not matters of luck, but rather that we cannot satisfy the parties' fundamental interest in making choices that genuinely shape their lives without accepting some of them, then the sense in which determinism implies that the inequalities *are* matters of luck will simply be beside the point.[13] Here again, what matters is only that the parties exercise

---

[11] Samuel Scheffler, "Choice, Circumstance, and the Value of Equality," in Samuel Scheffler, *Equality and Tradition* (Oxford University Press, 2010), p. 218. For related discussion, see Saul Smilansky, "Egalitarian Justice and the Importance of the Free Will Problem," *Philosophia* 25 (1997): 153–61.

[12] Gerald Cohen, "On the Currency of Egalitarian Justice," *Ethics* 99 (1989): 906–47, at 934.

[13] It will also be beside the point to object that a choice that is caused by antecedent events cannot *satisfy* a person's interest in living his own life effectively because such choice is not genuinely the agent's own. That objection might indeed have force against an argument which sought to ground our interest in living our lives effectively in some deeper imperative of self-realization. However, far from appealing to any such idea, I have based my claim that each person has such an interest on the far less contestable premises that each of us is a separate center of consciousness, and that

control going forward. Thus, instead of committing us to a conception of choice that requires some kind of contracausal freedom, our justification will allow us to accept one of the standard compatibilist conceptions. Although there is of course still a question about *which* compatibilist conception to accept, we can simply add this to the already lengthy list of questions whose answers depend on what is involved in living one's life effectively.

each person's consciousness has certain generic features that make it both possible and necessary for him to live in certain characteristic ways. Because these premises merely describe our subjectivity, they cannot be undermined by any facts about what causes it. Although the claim that everything that goes on within each center of consciousness is caused is (to say the least) hardly unproblematic, it is significant that even those philosophers who are most skeptical of our ability to make sense of consciousness within a naturalistic framework do not generally deny the relevance of experience to ethics.

CHAPTER 7

Coping with contingency

To render its members able to live their lives effectively, a society must allow their choices to play out in ways that leave different people with different amounts of various goods – including, sometimes, the good of being able to live effectively itself. This is the connection between distributive equality and choice-related inequality that luck egalitarians rightly discern but wrongly analyze and defend. But what, beyond being able to make choices that stick, does the ability to live one's life effectively involve, and to what level of it must societies elevate their citizens?

I

It is important to bear in mind that what we are after is not an analysis of some antecedently understood notion of effectiveness. As I am using it here, the phrase "living one's life effectively" is a term of art. Its function is to designate whichever dimension of the kind of life into which a normal human being's consciousness channels him (a) is not automatically present in every such life, but (b) bears a relation to what *is* automatically present that warrants its inclusion in each person's fundamental interest. In the previous chapter, I suggested that our lives must contain some such dimension because the activities into which our consciousness channels us incorporate standards of success that are not automatically met. But what, exactly, are those standards, and to what interests do they give rise?

To bring the issues into focus, it will be helpful to remind ourselves, first, of the fundamental assumptions that have been seen to structure our consciousness, and then, second, of the sorts of activities into which that consciousness channels us. For present purposes, the most important of the assumptions are that (1) we are embodied beings who exist in space as well as time; that (2) we will persist as embodied beings, and will retain our identities, for at least some period in the future; that (3) we have the power both to decide among sets of available actions and to implement whatever decisions we make; that (4) what we decide and do can have an impact both on our own lives and on the wider world; and that (5) we have reasons to act in some ways rather than others, and are often capable both of discerning those reasons and of basing our decisions on them. If we failed to make any of these assumptions, we would not be practical agents; but because we cannot avoid making any of them, we also cannot escape our agency.

Being a practical agent means confronting the world in certain characteristic ways. Because we cannot help thinking in terms of reasons, we cannot but form beliefs about which ends are worth seeking. Because achieving our ends requires adopting appropriate means, we must form plans to get what we want. Because our plans require implementation, we must act on them when the occasion arises. Thus, the activities into which our consciousness channels us must include (at least) the adoption of aims or ends, the formulation of plans designed to realize them, and the implementation of those plans. In making these distinctions, I do not mean to suggest that agents always, or even often, pass through discrete stages of weighing up pros and cons, settling on plans, and swinging into action. To the contrary, it is clear that real-world agency is a jumble – that we generally decide and act on the fly and then if pressed reconstruct our reasons as best we can. However, what this shows is not that we cannot usefully break agency down into component activities, but only that any resulting divisions will be analytical rather than chronological.

This crude taxonomy could obviously be refined in a number of ways. However, even without refinement, it clearly illustrates the ways in which the major components of practical agency – evaluating and adopting ends, forming plans for their realization, and executing those plans – are governed by different standards. Where the adoption of ends is concerned, the standards require the accurate identification of whatever aspects of the agent's situation are relevant and the appropriate weighting of the reasons each provides. Where planning is concerned, they require economy in the projected use of resources and accuracy in calculating what will lead to what. Where the execution of a plan is concerned, they require skill, resoluteness, and flexibility in the performance of the projected actions. In each case, to engage in the relevant activity is *ipso facto* to seek to satisfy the standards that it incorporates and by which it is defined. Thus, to live his life effectively, an agent must satisfy all three sets of standards: he must, over the course of time, accurately discern what he has reason to aim at, see what he needs to do to get it, and succeed at doing what needs to be done. This is, I think, a worthy and plausible schematic rendering of each person's most fundamental interest.[1]

II

I will turn shortly to the question of how this schema can best be filled in, and of the sorts of lives that it does and does not count as effective. However, before I do that, I want briefly to examine the schema's political implications. Given my claim that the good whose distribution matters most is the ability to live one's life effectively, what does this way of understanding effectiveness tell us about the state's distributive obligations?

The first thing it tells us is that the state cannot possibly be obligated to bring it about that each citizen *does* live his life effectively. To do this, the state would have to cause each citizen to adopt only those ends, and only those means of achieving his ends, that are in fact supported by the strongest reasons that his situation provides. However, far from living his life effectively, any citizen whose ends and activities were orchestrated in this way would not be living a life of his own at

---

[1] For another account that identifies a person's interests with his success at satisfying the standards that are internal to activities such as goal-seeking and believing, see Simon Keller, "Welfare as Success," *Nous* 43 (2009): 656–83. Keller, however, does not represent these activities as forced upon us by the assumptions around which our consciousness is structured; he acknowledges (though perhaps only for purposes of argument) the possibility of a person with no goals at all.

all. If, impossibly, the state could cause each citizen to adopt all and only those ends that were supported by the best (or good enough) reasons, and all and only those plans for achieving his ends that were best all things considered, then the ends and activities that its citizens pursued would not reflect their own assessments of their situations. Because a person cannot live his own life without having the leeway to make his own mistakes, it would be self-defeating for the state to try to cause him to live effectively. That is why I have been careful to say that the good with which the state must provide its citizens is only the *ability* to live their lives effectively.

Because the state's distributive obligations can extend only this far, it must be able to discharge them by doing no more than (a) creating the conditions under which each citizen is both competent and in a position to evaluate whatever reasons he has, and (b) providing each citizen with access to some suitable amount of resources and opportunities. However, when I say this, I do not mean to deny either that the state must take positive steps to enable its citizens to recognize and respond to the reasons provided by their situations or that it may favor some conceptions of the good over others. Although the issues here are tricky, I accept both claims, and before I proceed further I want briefly to explain why.

The obvious reason to insist that governments must take positive steps to enable citizens to appreciate their reasons is that no one can accurately assess the reasons that bear on either his possible ends or the possible ways of achieving them unless he knows whatever facts *provide* him with those reasons. This means that whatever else it does, the state must provide each citizen with enough education to give him access to the relevant facts. There is, of course, an intense ongoing debate about what a satisfactory curriculum must include, and this debate is often a lightning rod for the deeper disagreements that divide us. However, the broad idea that no one can navigate the modern world unless he is both literate and informed, and that the state is therefore obligated to educate all of its citizens up to some appropriate level, is common ground to all parties. This shared idea meshes nicely with what I have already said, and I will not belabor it here.

The harder question is whether the state's obligations in this area extend further. That they may is suggested by the fact that even the best-educated among us can, and often do, make a mess of our lives. Because knowledge is no substitute for sound reasoning and good judgment, it is tempting to infer that any government that seeks to enable its citizens to live their lives effectively must strive to elevate their judgment and reasoning skills as well as providing them with information. Moreover, as long as it is marshalled in support of techniques that do not seek to remake particular individuals, and that are directed exclusively at the processes through which habits of judgment and reasoning are formed, I think this inference is indeed warranted. There is, for example, nothing wrong with adding informal logic to the high school curriculum (although I have some doubts about its usefulness). More importantly, to whatever extent the prevailing social conditions cause some segments of the population to prize immediate gratification over longer-term benefit, the alteration of those conditions would be a large and obvious boon.[2]

But precisely because any such policies would have to be general and broad-gauged, they do not go to the heart of the matter. In the end, weighing possible ends and evaluating possible ways of achieving them are things we must do as individuals; and how well or badly we do them is a direct reflection of who we are. The good or bad judgment that any person exhibits is inseparable from his underlying combination of traits, tendencies, quirks, beliefs, and attitudes – his whole sensibility and cast of mind. Thus, to render particular individuals better at reasoning and judging, the state would often have to alter the characteristics that distort their current performance. However, when the aim of improving a person's habits of thought begins to call for alterations that touch on his selfhood, it quickly becomes repugnant.

---

[2] I have put this point cautiously because the thesis that there is a distinct culture of poverty is controversial. For defense of that thesis, see Michael Harrington, *The Other America* (New York: Macmillan, 1962) and Edward Banfield, *The Unheavenly City* (Boston: Little, Brown and Company, 1968); for criticism, see William Julius Wilson, *The Truly Disadvantaged* (University of Chicago Press, 1987) and Herbert Gans, *The War against the Poor: The Underclass and Antipoverty Policy* (New York: Basic Books, 1995).

If anything is more intrusive than preventing someone from living his own life, it is intervening to remake the person whose life is in question. It is, I think, no accident that many of the techniques that come to mind as ways of effecting such changes — "reeducation," behavior modification, pharmacological treatment, neurosurgical intervention — have a totalitarian flavor. But even if more acceptable techniques could be found, the end they served would remain objectionable. When the state creates the conditions under which good habits of judgment and reasoning can develop, it exhausts the only obligations that it can have in this area.

One further question warrants brief mention, and that is whether governments are ever justified in promoting particular conceptions of the good. As long as it avoids any overly intrusive attempts to alter anyone's habits of judgment, may the state try to induce its citizens to live in ways that it considers valuable rather than disvaluable? In my earlier book *Beyond Neutrality*,[3] I argued at length that such efforts are both legitimate and often justified. But isn't this inconsistent with my current claim that it is self-defeating for the state to try to cause someone to live his life effectively by taking over all of his important decisions?[4]

The answer, I think, is that although the two positions are indeed in some tension, there is a vast difference between a government that takes over all of a person's major decisions, or that seeks to reorder the personality structure from which his judgments spring, and one that merely alters selected elements of his option-set. I argued in *Beyond Neutrality* that governments can seek to promote the good in at least four ways: by providing incentives to engage in activities they consider valuable, by creating social forms that make such activities possible, by non-rationally conditioning citizens to prefer such activities, and by criminalizing activities they consider disvaluable. Of these four methods, the first two clearly do not threaten anyone's ability to live his own life effectively, while the third will remain minimally threatening

---

[3] George Sher, *Beyond Neutrality: Perfectionism and Politics* (Cambridge University Press, 1997).

[4] I am grateful to Anthony Carreras for pressing me to confront this objection.

as long as the conditioning is targeted at specific preferences and merely exploits the sorts of non-rational influences that would operate in any case. By contrast, the fourth way of promoting the good — attaching criminal penalties to disvaluable activities — may indeed appear to pose a threat, and so it is important to explain why it does not.

To see why criminalizing disvaluable activities need not reduce anyone's ability to live effectively, we need only remind ourselves of how limited and variable each person's options are to begin with. Although each of us is free to do many things, there are vastly more things that each is *not* free to do; and both lists are constantly being altered by both natural and social forces. This constant fluctuation makes it possible to envision a situation in which the natural forces that are at play in a neutral state turn out to narrow its citizens' options in a way that precisely matches the narrowing that a perfectionist state creates through its system of legal penalties. We can imagine, for example, that all the drugs whose use is criminalized within the perfectionist state are wiped out by a plant blight in the neutral one. If the citizens of the perfectionist state were rendered less able to live effectively by its legal prohibitions, then the citizens of the neutral state would have to be similarly affected by the plant blight. However, in fact, the citizens of the neutral state are clearly *not* rendered any less able to live effectively by the loss of their drugs. Thus, to be consistent, we must acknowledge that the citizens of the perfectionist state are also not rendered less able to live effectively by its legal prohibitions.

III

Bearing all this in mind, let us return to our schematic account of effectiveness. I have argued that the degree to which a person lives his life effectively, and thus too the degree to which he realizes his fundamental interest, is determined by how well he succeeds at satisfying the standards that are internal to the activities into which his form of consciousness channels him. To succeed at satisfying these standards, the person must set his ends, and must make and implement his plans, in ways that respond appropriately to whatever reasons his situation provides. Because our situations are constantly evolving, this conception of success is a dynamic one, and that fact has important implications both about what living one's life effectively comes to and about what the state must do to promote the ability to live that way. To bring these implications into the open, I now want to contrast my own account of success with a more static account that it superficially resembles. The alternative I have in mind is the "full theory of the good" that Rawls summarizes in the claim that "[t]he rational plan for a person determines his good"[5] (or, more cautiously, it is the theory that emerges under a certain perhaps contestable interpretation of that claim).

Like his theory of justice, Rawls's full theory of the good contains a hypothetical element. It identifies a person's good not with his getting what he does want, but rather with his getting what he would want if he were accurately to envision all the different courses that his life might take.[6] As Rawls himself writes,

> we can say that the rational plan for a person . . . is the plan that would be decided upon as the outcome of careful reflection in which the agent reviewed, in the light of all the relevant facts, what it would be like to carry out these plans and thereby ascertained the course of action that would best realize his more fundamental desires.[7]

At the moment of choice, which presumably occurs early in a person's life, "the agent's knowledge of his situation and the consequences of carrying out each plan is presumed to be accurate and complete," and "no relevant circumstances are left out of account."[8] Armed with this knowledge, the agent simultaneously envisions each distinct life that he might live — that is, each life that is represented by a beginning-to-end branch of a decision tree that originates in the present and

---

[5] John Rawls, *A Theory of Justice* (Cambridge, MA: Harvard University Press, 1971), p. 408.

[6] "[A] rational plan is one that would be selected if certain conditions were fulfilled. The criterion of the good is hypothetical in a way similar to the criterion of justice" (*ibid.*, p. 421).

[7] *Ibid.*, p. 417.   [8] *Ibid.*

at each moment divides as many times as he then has distinct available actions. Of these different possible lives, the agent's good is said to consist of whichever beginning-to-end branch he would most prefer.

Although Rawls evaluates plans in terms of their ability to realize fundamental desires rather than rational ends, this difference is not significant because he holds, in effect, that the things an agent finds himself wanting most just *are* his rational ends.[9] However, what is significant for our purposes is that, when Rawls speaks of rational plans, he always uses the definite article. Instead of entertaining the possibility that what counts as the rational plan that determines a person's good might change as his circumstances shift, Rawls consistently emphasizes the need for continuity. He views the later events in a person's life not as giving him reason to adjust his original plan, but rather as considerations that he must take into account when forming that plan. We are to choose the single plan that binds the different stages of our lives together, and we are to do so with an eye to shaping our future desires so that they mesh with our present overall aims. Although the plan as chosen may not be completely detailed – Rawls writes that a person's rational plan "consists of a hierarchy of plans, the more specific subplans being filled in at the appropriate time"[10] – each subsequent temporal standpoint is allowed only subordinate authority. This suggests that at every time after the imagined original review, the person's life is worsened by each major deviation from whichever aspects of the plan are already filled in.

But if this is what Rawls has in mind, then his account has implications that diverge widely from our considered judgments about what counts as a good or successful life. To bring out these divergent implications, let us consider the simple example of a person who earlier in his life declined an opportunity to invest heavily in Microsoft. This opportunity, had the agent taken it, would have made him extremely

---

9   Thus, he writes that "[s]ometimes there is no way to avoid having to assess the relative intensity of our desires . . . It is clearly left to the agent himself to decide what it is that he most wants and to judge the comparative importance of his several ends" (*ibid.*, p. 416).

10 *Ibid.*, p. 410.

rich, and would have made possible a life that differed immeasurably from his actual modest one. That life would have contained far
more of what he originally viewed as most worth seeking, and in fact
would have coincided exactly with the most favored beginning-to-
end branch of his decision-tree. By contrast, his actual humble life is
very different. It contains a good deal of hardship, involves entirely
different activities and a wholly different cast of characters, and is
unlike the most favored branch in every important particular. If the
goodness of a person's life depends on how closely it approximates
his Rawlsian rational plan, then this person must be judged to have
fared very poorly. However, in fact, that judgment is unwarranted. A
person's life can hardly be blighted simply by its radical divergence
from another that he would once have preferred. Instead, the degree
to which the agent's actual life is a good one, and the degree to which
his fundamental interests are realized, will evidently depend on facts
about the case that have not yet been specified. But which facts are
these, and what determines their relevance?

The natural answer – and, not coincidentally, the one that is suggested by the dynamic account I am proposing – is that they are facts
about the choices that the agent makes *after* the Microsoft decision.
Intuitively, what matters in a case like this is not so much whether
he takes advantage of his single big opportunity, but rather how
well he handles the unfolding sequence of later choice-situations into
which the world and his earlier decisions funnel him. On the dynamic
account, moreover, this is only to be expected; for because the internal
aims of the activities into which our consciousness channels us must
continue to be our aims whenever we *are* conscious, they cannot be
definitively achieved or frustrated by our success or failure at implementing the plan that we have reason to adopt at any single moment.
Instead, if at t2 we can no longer carry out the plan whose adoption
was dictated by the relevant aims at t1 – if, for example, we have
missed a flight that we needed to catch in order to take advantage
of a one-time opportunity – then at t2 those aims will simply dictate
the adoption of a different plan. This new plan – the notorious plan
B – may be designed to maximize the achievement of some entirely
different combination of rational ends, and may dictate a sequence of

actions which in no way resembles the original. That does not prevent us from saying that the effectiveness with which a person lives his life depends on his success at achieving his rational ends, but it does mean that that form of success cannot be wedded to the implementation of any single plan.[11]

Thus, it is hardly surprising that the fit, or lack of it, between a person's actual life and his Rawlsian rational plan tells us very little about how effectively he has lived (or, to put the point in Rawls's terms, about how well his life has gone). In our Microsoft example, the plan that the agent would have chosen before the Microsoft stock became available is no more authoritative than the plan he would have chosen immediately after the opportunity to purchase the stock was lost. However, there is of course no reason to privilege this second plan either, since just as the agent's life cannot be blighted by his single decision not to purchase Microsoft, so too can it not be blighted by the first bad decision that he makes after that. Because our lives are lived over time, the overall effectiveness with which we live them must depend in some complex way on the effectiveness with which we respond to the new situations that are constantly arising at different moments within them. In saying this, I do not mean to deny that the goodness or overall effectiveness of a person's life can be diminished

---

[11] There is also a further problem with Rawls's full theory, and that is that what would lead someone to favor a given beginning-to-end branch of his decision tree is often a fact that is too singular to have any normative significance. Thus, to cite a crass, stock example, an agent with complete knowledge of the consequences of every action he can possibly perform must recognize that traveling directly to Las Vegas and betting all his savings on a certain sequence of spins of a certain roulette wheel will make him immensely rich, and thus will make possible a life that differs immeasurably from the one that he will in fact live. He must also recognize that attending a certain party, or traveling on a certain day to Topeka or Cairo or a town in Uttar Pradesh, will enable him to meet the woman with whom he is uniquely best suited to live his life, and that attempting an apparently useless and risky medical procedure will lead to an advance in heart surgery that rockets him to the top of his profession. These rich and rewarding lives, and innumerable others, will be arrayed before him, and we may suppose that he would much prefer them to his more ordinary life of financial insecurity, intermittent marital discord, and routine medical practice. Nevertheless, neither the strength of this preference nor the magnitude of the gap between these lives and his own tells us anything about the goodness of his life as it actually unfolds.

if its different segments display the wrong sort of trajectory or lack narrative coherence. Whether and in what sense this is so are matters of ongoing debate.[12] My point, rather, is that to whatever extent coherence or trajectory does matter, any aspects of the agent's past that now give him reason to move forward in one way rather than another do so not in virtue of any plans that he previously formed, but rather as elements of a new situation in the light of which his previous plans are up for review.[13]

IV

Although this account preserves the connection between the notion of a plan and that of living one's life effectively, it radically transforms the way in which we must think of this connection. Instead of allowing us to construe plans simply as inert templates against which to evaluate the events in people's lives, it compels us to regard them as the propositional contents of the active responses that people make to the specific and highly mutable circumstances that they encounter. This implies, *contra* Rawls, that what really determines the success of

---

[12] For relevant discussion, see J. David Velleman, "Well-Being and Time" in his *The Possibility of Practical Reason* (Oxford University Press, 2000, pp. 56–84); Anntui Kauppinen, "Meaningfulness and Time," *Philosophy and Phenomenological Research* 84 (2012): 345–77; and Jason R. Raibly, "Welfare over Time and the Case for Holism," *Philosophical Papers* 41 (2012): 239–65.

[13] At first glance, this claim may appear to conflict with the truism that adopting a plan means settling questions about what to do that would otherwise remain open. However, while we often do have reason to follow through on our intentions without further consideration – for contrasting explanations of this, see David Velleman, *Practical Reflection* (Princeton University Press, 1989) and Michael Bratman, *Intention, Plans, and Practical Reason* (Cambridge, MA: Harvard University Press, 1987) – the considerations that provide us with that reason establish only a presumption that can be overridden by a variety of factors. For example, in his recent book *Willing, Wanting, Waiting* (Oxford University Press, 2009), Richard Holton plausibly suggests that it can be rational to reconsider an intention if we believe that circumstances have changed in a way that defeats the intention's purpose, if we believe it can no longer be carried out, or if we believe that acting on it will cause suffering that we did not originally envision. When I speak of the review to which an agent's plans are subject, I mean one that is justified by some aspect of the way his life has developed since he formed the plan.

a person's life is not its relation to a favored abstract structure that describes an optimal sequence of acts and their sequellae, but rather certain facts about the dynamic process through which he forms and reforms intentions which in their turn *embed* an evolving sequence of such abstract structures.[14] This implication is significant because it reflects, and compels us to acknowledge, the crucial fact that lives are, above all, *lived*.

It is a military cliché that no battle plan survives the first contact with the enemy. Just so, but far more generally, no life-plan that is detailed enough to provide a useful criterion of effectiveness is likely to survive contact with the innumerable surprises, obstacles, windfalls, shocks, and reversals that together make up a human life. To drive this point home, it will be helpful to survey a small sample of these disruptive contingencies. Thus, imagine a person with a definite picture of the way he wants his future life to go – it can be as detailed or loose, and as bland or outré, as you like – and then imagine the adjustments he must make if:

1. his company announces that it is going to relocate from Newark, NJ, to Chicopee, MA;
2. he develops multiple sclerosis;
3. the paintings he does as a hobby attract the attention of a dealer and begin to command high prices on the international market;
4. his wife becomes obsessed with her charity work and his marriage degenerates into an endless series of fights;
5. a balloon angiogram reveals that he needs open-heart surgery;
6. his new boss subjects him to persistent humiliation and harrassment;
7. the house next door is converted to an apartment for students whose parties keep him up all night;
8. he wins the Megabucks;
9. his daughter is arrested on a serious drug charge; or

---

[14] For related criticism of the role that Rawls assigns to rational life-plans, see David Heyd and G. Franklin Miller, "Life Plans: Do They Give Meaning to Our Lives?," *The Monist* 93 (2010): 17–37, and Charles Larmore, "The Idea of a Life Plan," *Social Philosophy and Policy* 16 (1999): 96–112.

10. he discovers on his fifty-eighth birthday that his retirement fund has lost two-thirds of its value.

In each such case, an agent who wishes to achieve as much as possible of what he views as most important may have reason to modify drastically, if not altogether abandon, his original plans.

These cases remind us that whatever plans we make are hostage to innumerable contingencies that we can neither foresee nor control. However, to leave things here would be to overlook the significance of another, deeper level of contingency – one that doesn't so much disrupt plans as set the parameters within which they are formed. Think, for example, of the impact on a person's life of his being

11. raised by parents who attach little importance to education (constantly provide him with stimulation, are in and out of prison);

12. homely and sexually unattractive (instantly likable, socially maladroit);

13. comfortable only in an area of the country where there is no work;

14. alive at a time and place with a functioning power grid;

15. born and raised during a depression;

16. subject to depression;

17. in the right place, at the right time, to meet his future wife (his future best friend, the bad influence who will lead him astray);

18. not quite distinguished enough to secure a tenure-track appointment;

19. talented in ways for which there is no (a great deal of) demand; or

20. just under five feet tall.

And, at a deeper level yet, there is the vertigo-inducing concatenation of vanishingly improbable past events in the absence of any one of which the world that is one's consciousness would not now exist at all.

Bearing all this in mind, let us return to our guiding question of how best to understand the idea of living one's life effectively. Building on what has been said, we can now see that this is largely a matter of coping with contingency. To appreciate the ends we have most reason to pursue, and to adopt the best overall means to their joint achievement, we must tailor our aspirations to the innumerable contingencies that determine which paths are open to us.[15] This means adjusting our aspirations in light of what we can realistically hope to accomplish, and it also means altering those aspirations, and the plans by which we hope to realize them, when our circumstances change in ways that we could not foresee. This is not to say that people never have reason to pursue ends they know they are unlikely to achieve, but it is to say that any criterion of effectiveness that is supplied by the internal aims of deliberation and planning must be weighted heavily in the direction of both realism and flexibility. To live our lives effectively, we often must trim our ends to fit the available means.

V

In arguing that living one's life effectively is largely a matter of coping with contingency, I have relied mainly on examples that illustrate the impact of contingency on our reasons to pursue self-regarding goals. However, in offering these examples, I do not mean to suggest that all rational ends are either self-regarding or perpetually subject to alteration as our circumstances shift. I am happy to agree that we also have reasons that are rooted in a universal and timeless morality —

---

[15] Compare Ronald Dworkin: "If we . . . treat living well as responding in the right way to one's situation, then we must treat some of the circumstances in which a particular person lives . . . as parameters that help define what a good performance of living would be for him . . . These circumstances include our health, our physical powers, our tenure of life, our material resources, our friendships and associations, our commitments and traditions of family and race and nation, the constitution and legal system under which we live, the intellectual and literary and philosophical opportunities and standards offered by our language and culture, and thousands of other aspects of our world as well": Ronald Dworkin, *Sovereign Virtue* (Cambridge, MA: Harvard University Press, 2000), p. 260. Because Dworkin wishes to avoid the conclusion that any and every life that any person might live is equally good, he is unwilling to treat *all* the facts about a person and his situation as parameters. However, on my account, there is no need to exclude any of these facts, since even if we include them all, a person will not live well (or, in my terms, effectively) if the plans he forms in light of his situation do not sufficiently achieve his generic aims. For this reason, I am free to treat all of the factors on Dworkin's list as what he calls parameters.

reasons to deal fairly and honestly with others, to spare them needless pain, and so on – and that further reasons are provided by the intrinsic or inherent goodness of certain types of activities or outcomes. Where such reasons are concerned, our contingent circumstances are relevant only insofar as they determine which acts would be fair and honest and which activities or outcomes would have the relevant good-making features. But even if we all have good reason to put morality and excellence first, each of us is also committed to many more personal projects involving family, politics, religion and the like, and unexpected turns of events are always capable of altering the reasons that underwrite these. A sudden death, a new relationship or enthusiasm, a loss of faith – all such changes, and indefinitely many others, can provide new reasons to follow new paths. And given the endless variety of ways in which people's circumstances can change, the variety of paths that they can have reason to follow must be endless as well.

Because of this, there are many different kinds of lives that can satisfy the proposed criteria of effectiveness. Given a suitable constellation of internal and external factors, a person may satisfy the standards that govern his deliberative activities by living a life that is driven, relaxed, sybaritic, ascetic, social, reclusive, domestic, adventurous, self-promoting, or self-sacrificing. He may also satisfy those standards by living a life that displays some combination of those traits, either simultaneously or in turn. The flexibility of this conception of effectiveness is a virtue because any account that confined the sorts of lives that can satisfy a person's most fundamental interest to a few simple patterns would be implausible on its face.

It may be wondered, though, whether my account is a bit *too* flexible; for by linking effectiveness as closely as I do to the accommodation of contingency, I may seem to imply that a government can render its citizens sufficiently able to live their lives effectively without providing much in the way of resources or opportunities. This objection is important both because it would be damaging if successful and because the reasons for its failure contain important clues about the level of provision that *would* be sufficient. For both reasons, it will be useful to consider the objection in some detail.

To bring it into focus, we need only retrace the argument's course. I have argued that a just society is one whose members are sufficiently able to live their lives effectively, and that the relevant form of effectiveness involves, among other things, the ability to recognize the ends that one in fact has most reason to seek. I have argued, as well, that the considerations that determine which ends an agent has most reason to seek include facts about what he can realistically hope to accomplish — that, for example, a person might rationally aspire to be a champion high-jumper but not to jump over the moon, or to build an ultra-light airplane but not a cyclotron. Prominent among the considerations that determine the limits of what an agent can reasonably hope to accomplish are the resources and opportunities to which he has access. But, notoriously, a person's access to resources and opportunities is heavily dependent on the very social institutions whose justice is currently at issue.

From the premises that societies are just when they elevate all citizens to appropriate levels of ability to live effectively, that an agent's ability to live effectively depends on his ability to achieve his rational ends, and that an agent's rational ends are limited by what he can realistically hope to accomplish, it follows that even societies that distribute resources and opportunities unequally may sometimes qualify as just. Consider, for example, a society in which Les has access to significantly fewer resources and opportunities than does Morey. By the proposed criterion, Les and Morey may still be equally able to live their lives effectively if the impact of Les's having fewer resources and opportunities is simply to give him reason to reduce his aspirations by a commensurate amount. If Morey can afford an education at a top law school while the best that Les can do is a year at the local community college, then Morey's rational ends may include a career in corporate law or high finance while Les's may extend no further than a steady job at an auto body shop. Assuming that Morey and Les are both able to achieve their rational ends, and that nothing else prevents either one from living his life effectively, the prevailing economic inequality will not render their society unjust.

The fact that a theory of distributive justice allows a measure of economic inequality is not necessarily a strike against it. Any theory that seeks the equal distribution of something other than resources is likely to tolerate such inequalities, and, at least since the publication of Dworkin's landmark essays, it has been widely agreed that in order to reconcile equality with choice, a defender of equality of resources must do so as well. However, what is disturbing is the absence of any limits on the amounts of social and economic inequality that seem consistent with distributive justice as I have represented it. Imagine a society as stratified and oppressive as you like – one in which a tiny minority of the population lives in baronial splendor and exercises complete control over the political process, but in which vastly greater numbers subsist in abject poverty from which they have no hope of escape. In this sort of all-too-familiar society, the poverty and lack of opportunity of the masses will make it reasonable for them to restrict their ambitions to a few very modest ends (scrounging enough food to last the week, keeping their children alive until they are grown) that they have some hope of attaining. If their aspirations are sufficiently modest, then even the most downtrodden may seem as able as their wealthy overlords to realize their rational ends in ways that count as living one's life effectively.[16] But even if they are, it would be a bad joke to say that their society is therefore just.

Because any theory that had this implication would be unacceptable on its face, it is important to stress that my own account implies no such thing. The reason, in brief, is that while being able to live one's life effectively does require appreciating the limits on what one can achieve and tailoring one's ends to the available means, it also involves much else. Indeed, given what has been said, we can distinguish at least four ways in which the effectiveness of the members of our imagined society is likely to be gravely compromised.

[16] Despite Rawls's claim that a person's rational life-plan is what determines his good, the fact that those with fewer resources and opportunities than others have reason to pursue less ambitious plans poses no comparable problem for him. The reason, in brief, is that he does not take this conception of a person's good to play any role in shaping the distributive principles that should govern the design of a society's institutions. For Rawls, a society's justice depends exclusively on the way it distributes wealth, opportunities, and other elements of his "thin theory" – that is, goods which are useful in the pursuit of many different ends, and which are therefore presumed to be of equal worth to all persons.

First, because the standards that determine effectiveness govern cognitive activities such as recognizing one's situation, envisioning alternatives, weighing reasons, and forming and revising plans, they require a clarity of mind and a breadth of imagination that poverty and oppression can all too easily suppress. Someone who is malnourished and desperate is in no condition to think clearly about his future; someone who is resigned and hopeless is not well positioned to do what is needed to improve his situation.

Second, because living a life is an active enterprise, it requires a sphere of efficacy and control that grinding poverty is bound to undermine. Those with extremely limited resources and opportunities have very few options, and are constantly forced to do whatever will meet their immediate needs. They are little different from Joseph Raz's Hounded Woman, who "shares [an] island with a fierce carnivorous animal which perpetually hunts for her," who is "taxed to the limits by her struggle to remain alive," and who "never has a chance to do or even think of anything other than how to escape from the beast."[17] Their lives are, in a real sense, not their own to live.

Third, lives of poverty are very *hard* lives. Even in the United States, the poor are often restricted to rundown, dangerous areas which lack both amenities and basic services; and in many stratified and oppressive societies, things are far worse. Work, if available at all, is repetitive and unpleasant and consumes most waking hours; untreated illness causes much suffering. I have argued at some length that no single hardship can undermine the effectiveness with which a person lives his life, but I have also argued that the criteria of effectiveness must accommodate the demands of human psychology. To be able to live his life effectively, a person must have access to some creature comforts, some relaxation, and some of the other things that humans find enjoyable and pleasant. This condition is not met when hardship is unrelenting and the future offers no prospect of relief.

Moreover, just as a person cannot live his life effectively if he entirely lacks access to the things that all humans enjoy, he also cannot do so if he entirely lacks access to activities that *he in particular* would

---

[17] Joseph Raz, *The Morality of Freedom* (Oxford University Press, 1986), p. 374.

find congenial. Someone who must devote all his energies simply to surviving may act with great resourcefulness and ingenuity, but even if he does, his life will hardly be his own. Thus, the fourth and final way in which our downtrodden population will lack the ability to live their lives effectively is that they will not have the leeway to formulate or pursue projects of their own devising.

Given all this, we need not linger over the worry that the proposed account will compel us to accept even the grossest forms of social injustice. The harder question, though, is what to say about the indefinitely many social arrangements that are far less extreme than the ones just described, yet under which the resources and opportunities on which people can draw remain very unequally distributed. Of these different social arrangements, some but not others will presumably enable each of the citizens who live under them to live his life effectively. But where, exactly, should we draw this line, and on what basis should we draw it there rather than elsewhere?

CHAPTER 8

Enough is enough

I have argued that a society's primary distributive obligation is to render each of its members sufficiently able to live his own life effectively; and I have suggested, though not yet argued, that for each person that ability has some upper limit. Like any sufficiency view, mine needs to be backed by an explanation of where on the relevant continuum we should set the threshold. However, because the ability to live one's life effectively depends on a number of factors that come in degrees, some internal to the agent and some not, I will not be able to identify or defend the threshold until I have specified which continuum *is* the relevant one. That, accordingly, is my first task.

I

To satisfy its obligation to render its citizens sufficiently able to live their lives effectively, the state must render each of them sufficiently able to satisfy the standards that are built into the activities of setting ends and formulating and implementing plans for their achievement; and to do that, it must cause each citizen to attain a suitable level of education, opportunity, resources, and quality of judgment. Thus, on this account, there are two distinct (sets of) sufficiency thresholds: namely, (1) the level of overall ability to live effectively to which the state must elevate each citizen, and (2) the levels of education, opportunity, and the rest with which it must provide each citizen. Because these thresholds are located on different continua, there is an obvious question about how we can best order our thinking about them.

The two most eligible approaches are bottom-up and top-down. On the bottom-up approach, we begin with an independent specification of the conditions under which a person is sufficiently able to realize his fundamental interest in living his life effectively – one that does not presuppose anything about any of the other thresholds – and we then go on to specify the further thresholds by asking which levels of education, opportunity, resources, and judgment a person must attain in order to reach this one. By contrast, on the top-down approach, we begin with an independent specification of the levels of education, opportunity, resources, and judgment to which the state must elevate each citizen – one that again does not presuppose anything about any other threshold – and we then go on to identify the effectiveness threshold with whatever level of ability to live effectively the attainment of these thresholds makes possible. Of the two alternatives, the bottom-up approach offers the advantage of extending the argument from the foundations of our moral equality which I began in Chapter 5, while the top-down approach offers the compensating advantage of being far more concrete and easy to grasp. For both approaches, the central task is to provide a well-motivated independent specification of the threshold with which we begin.

But how, in either case, can that task be discharged? On what basis can we draw a principled line between those who are sufficiently able to live their lives effectively and those who are not? And how, alternatively, can we draw a principled line between those who do and do not have enough opportunity, enough education, access to enough resources, or good enough judgment? Generalizing from questions like these, Paula Casal has written that

> [g]iven the importance sufficientarians attach to individuals having "enough," perhaps the most pressing problem they face is to specify that idea in a principled way that provides determinate and plausible guidance for distributive decision makers.[1]

---

[1] Paula Casal, "Why Sufficiency Is Not Enough," *Ethics* 117 (2007): 296–326. For another version of this criticism, see Richard Arneson, "Distributive Ethics and Basic Capability Equality: 'Good Enough' Is not Enough," in *Capabilities Equality: Basic Issues and Problems*, ed. Alexander Kaufman (New York: Routledge, 2006), pp. 17–43.

It's a fair criticism, and, in my opinion, one that sufficientarians have thus far not succeeded in meeting.[2]

But to say that the criticism has not been met is not to say that it cannot be. I believe, in fact, that the machinery developed here provides a way of answering it, and that it does so for both the bottom-up and the top-down approach. To anticipate the much longer story I am about to tell: for the bottom-up approach, the threshold coincides with the upper limit of each person's ability to live his life effectively, while for the top-down approach, the thresholds for resources, education, and the rest are established through independent examinations of the ways in which each good contributes to a person's ability to live effectively. Because each approach provides a way of deriving the threshold that the other approach takes as its starting point, a natural way to evaluate my versions of the two approaches is to ask whether their results match.

II

Let us begin with the top-down approach, which seeks to establish thresholds both for the traditional goods of resources, opportunities, and education and for the less traditional goods of being able to judge and reason well. Of the entries on this list, each can be ranged on its own continuum: a person can have many opportunities but few resources, many resources but little education, much education but

---

[2] The two most important attempts are those of Harry Frankfurt and Elizabeth Anderson. In his ground-breaking essay "Equality as a Moral Ideal" (in his *The Importance of What We Care About* (Cambridge University Press, 1988), pp. 134–58), Frankfurt writes that "[t]o say that a person has enough money means that he is content, or that it is reasonable for him to be content, with having no more money than he has" (p. 152). In her equally ground-breaking "What Is the Point of Equality?" (*Ethics* 109 (1999): pp. 287–337), Anderson argues that "everyone [must] have access to enough resources to avoid being oppressed by others and to function as an equal in civil society" (p. 320). For criticism of Frankfurt's criterion, see Casal, "Why Sufficiency Is Not Enough," p. 313. For an argument that "the . . . Anderson view that democratic equality is fundamental and the distribution of resources and opportunities and the like should be set so as best to promote democratic equality gets matters upside down," see Richard Arneson, "Luck Egalitarianism: An Interpretation and Defense," *Philosophical Topics* 32 (2004): 1–20.

poor judgment, and so on. Because it may or may not be possible to consolidate these continua, this plurality of goods does not by itself commit us to any set number of thresholds. However, it does suggest that we must settle this issue before we can advance to the question of what might determine the location of any relevant threshold.

Of the available solutions, the most straightforward is simply to maintain that there are as many distinct thresholds as there are goods of which each citizen must have a sufficient amount.[3] This will of course multiply both the number of continua on which we must draw dividing lines and the number of principled explanations of those divisions that we must offer; but neither complication seems particularly threatening. What does tell heavily against the proposal, though, is the fact that at least two of the goods in question, resources and opportunities, seem too closely related to have independent thresholds. One way to see this is to notice that a person with fewer resources than another may be no less advantaged if his greater range of opportunities allows him to do things – travel, grow food, get an education – on which the other must expend resources. Another is to remind ourselves that opportunities can be converted *into* resources – that, for example, an offer of admission to a prestigious law school may lead to higher earnings afterwards – and vice versa. For these reasons and others, the resource and opportunity continua, and so too the resource and opportunity thresholds, seem too interdependent to be distinct.

Generalizing from this, we may be tempted to consolidate all of the goods on our list into a single supergood, and to say that how much of that supergood any given person has is some complex function of his amount of each component good. By proceeding in this way, we would gain the advantage of having to draw and justify only a single line on a single continuum. The simplification would of course come at a cost, since, to achieve it, we would have to specify and defend the complex function that takes us from the component goods to the

[3] This is Martha Nussbaum's approach. In her book *Creating Capabilities* (Cambridge, MA: Harvard University Press, 2011) Nussbaum argues both that "[a]t a bare minimum, an ample threshold level of ten Central Capabilities is required," and that "respect for human dignity requires that citizens be placed above an ample (specified) threshold of capability, in all ten of those areas" (pp. 32, 36).

supergood. However, if the proposal were otherwise acceptable, then that problem might not be decisive.

But, in fact, the proposal is *not* otherwise defensible; for the remaining goods on our list do not admit the sorts of trade-offs that resources and opportunities allow. Unlike a deficit of resources or opportunities, which may be offset by a surplus of the other member of the pair, a deficit of education, judgment, or reasoning ability *cannot* be offset by a surplus of any other good. If someone is either illiterate or very ignorant, he is no less likely to squander a large stock of resources or opportunities than a small one; if someone cannot think logically, appreciate his limitations, or project the likely consequences of his actions, he is likely to waste his education as well as his opportunities and resources. Thus, where education, judgment, and reasoning ability are concerned, we do seem to be dealing with thresholds on independent continua.

Because neither the many- nor the single-threshold view seems plausible, I will opt for an intermediate view. With the single-threshold view, I will assume that resources and opportunities are sufficiently interchangeable to be ranked on a single continuum, and thus to have a single threshold. However, with the multi-threshold view, I will take education, judgment, and reasoning to fall on separate continua, and thus to have separate thresholds. Of the latter thresholds, I will assume that at least one must set a floor to the amount that each person must know (education), and that at least one other must specify the lowest acceptable level of proficiency at *using* what one knows (judgment, reasoning). Although both categories are obviously very broad, the question of whether further distinctions are needed – whether, for example, we need to separate thresholds for numeracy and literacy – is not one I will try to answer here.

Instead, let us turn to the question of where to set the thresholds we have already distinguished. To what minimum levels of resources and opportunities, education, and judgment and reasoning must the state elevate each citizen? And how, in each case, can we justify setting the minimum just there and not higher or lower?

At least in theory, the question about education is not that hard to answer. To live effectively, a person must be able to take advantage of the opportunities and resources to which he has access, and to do that, he must know various things and have various skills.[4] Thus, to identify what the schools must teach in order to render students *able* to live effectively, we need only ask what the requisite knowledge and skills involve. This of course does not tell us how much of any skill a person must have or how deep any form of knowledge must go; for there is probably no addition in either area that would not bring *some* increase in his ability to take advantage of his opportunities and resources. However, the rate of increase seems likely to drop off sharply once a person achieves basic literacy and numerical competence, a working knowledge of the core academic subjects, and a mastery of the main practicalities of modern life; and if it does, then we may naturally locate the threshold at or just beyond the point or stretch on the continuum at which the dropoff occurs.[5]

The question of where to set the reasoning and judgment threshold requires a different approach; for the kind of judgment that we exercise when we deliberate about which ends are worth seeking, and about how to reconcile competing worthwhile ends and deal with the ever-shifting obstacles to their achievement, is very different from any academic skill. It often requires an assessment of (among other things) the motives and characters of those with whom we must interact, the time it will take to do various things, the probable outcomes of events ranging from home improvement projects to governmental policies, and the relative weights of the radically different sorts of

---

[4] This is, of course, hardly the only important purpose that education serves. Two obvious others are, first, to enrich people's lives and, second, to prepare them for full participation in democratic governance. For discussion of the implications of the latter aim, see Amy Gutmann, *Democratic Education* (Princeton University Press, 1987).

[5] An important complication here is that education is in part a positional good, and that how much it contributes to a person's effectiveness can therefore depend on how much of it others have. So, for example, the amount of extra opportunity that a person gains from acquiring a given skill, or a given type of degree, depends on how many others also have that skill or that type of degree. Given this dependency, the need to bring everyone above the sufficiency threshold for resources and opportunities may exert pressure in the direction of certain forms of educational equality. For interesting discussion, see Harry Brighouse and Adam Swift, "Equality, Priority, and Positional Goods," *Ethics* 116 (2006): 471–97.

considerations that are bound to tell for and against the alternatives in any decision of any moment. As was suggested in the previous chapter, each person has his own ways of making these complicated assessments, and these patterns of thought are too deeply rooted in his character and cast of mind to be subject to legitimate alteration by his government. The state may and should create conditions that favor the development of good habits of reasoning and judgment, but even if it does, different people will benefit from these conditions to different degrees. Because people vary greatly in both psychology and native ability, there is no single level of proficiency to which the state may hope to elevate each citizen's judgment. Instead, the threshold for each person must simply be the level that he in fact reaches when his habits of reasoning and judgment develop under favorable conditions.

Although much more could obviously be said, the issues that are raised by the education and judgment/reasoning thresholds do not seem unmanageable. By contrast, the question of where to set the resource/opportunity threshold is more theoretically challenging. Because we are now exploring the top-down approach, we cannot simply identify that threshold with whatever combined amounts of resources and opportunities a person must have in order to be sufficiently able to live his life effectively. This does not mean that we cannot base our specification of the threshold on the claim that each person *has* a fundamental interest in living his life effectively, but it does prevent us from arguing that having some specified amount of resources and opportunities is necessary for reaching some distinct threshold of effectiveness. Thus, the question we must now ask is how else we might move from the claim that each person has a fundamental interest in living his life effectively to a specification of the amounts of resources and opportunities that the state must make available to its citizens.

III

In ordinary discourse, claims about sufficiency are always relative to contextually supplied aims. To say that we have enough gas in the tank is to say that we have enough to get us to our destination, and to say we have enough food is to say that we can satisfy our hunger. Along similar lines, we might try getting from our premise that each person has a fundamental interest in living his life effectively to a conclusion about how many resources and opportunities he must have by arguing that having a certain combined amount of these goods is necessary for achieving certain effectiveness-related goals. But to which goals, exactly, might our fundamental interest give rise?

Because a person's actions reflect his assessments of his reasons for acting, and because an effective agent is one who successfully acts for reasons that he has successfully identified as *calling* for action, one possible answer is that an effective agent must be able to achieve whichever of his actual goals he has good reason to seek. However, we have already seen that this answer is hopeless because a person's resources and opportunities are themselves a part of what *determines* which goals he has good reason to seek. When someone lacks the resources or opportunities to accomplish a particular goal, the rational thing for him to do, and thus what he will do if he is deliberating soundly, is often simply to replace it with another. Because a person's rational ends depend on the resources and opportunities to which he *does* have access, we cannot without circularity invoke his rational ends to specify the level of resources and opportunities to which he *should* have access. Nor, for obvious reasons, can we drop the reference to rationality, and simply take the level of resources and opportunities to which a person should have access to be the one that enables him to accomplish *whichever* goals he actually happens to have.

There is, however, a more promising possibility, which emerges when we remind ourselves that the goals to whose achievement a person's resources and opportunities are instrumental are not restricted to either of the categories just mentioned. An alternative class of goals, which looms large in many people's actual lives, involves the acquisition of *further* resources or opportunities. We are able to entertain these further goals because each person's level of resources and opportunities provides him with a measure of leverage over both the amounts of these goods he can have in the future and (therefore) the range of future goals that he will be able reasonably to pursue. Because such leverage is itself a matter of degree, it provides an alternative metric in terms of which we might express the minimum levels of resources and opportunities to which the state is obligated to elevate its citizens. Moreover, by shifting over to this metric, we will open up new possibilities for arriving at a principled specification of the relevant threshold.

These new possibilities arise because a person's leverage varies with the amounts of resources and opportunities that he already commands. Roughly speaking, the more resources or opportunities someone has, the better his prospects for increasing his stock further. From this generalization, it follows that anyone with any initial leverage can initiate a sequence of actions that is designed to take him, albeit perhaps in a lengthy series of steps, from his current level of resources and opportunities to some higher level. However, it also follows that if the beginning level is low enough, then climbing significantly higher is likely to take a long time and to require both cleverness and perseverance. In addition, especially in the early stages of the sequence, the agent will be vulnerable to unforeseen setbacks that can absorb his meager resources and that may thus slow or even reverse his progress. If the requisite efforts and adjustments are sufficiently difficult, protracted, or uncertain, they will either fall beyond the agent's capacities or else be so demanding as to be unreasonable to expect of him.

Because the ease with which a person is able to acquire further resources and opportunities is directly proportional to his current levels of these goods, there must be some point (or, more realistically, some stretch) on the resource/opportunity continuum to which an agent who falls below it cannot reasonably be expected to advance on his own, but from which an agent who is at or above it *can* reasonably be expected to advance on his own. This point or stretch has a normative significance that the others lack, and I now want to argue that it just *is* the threshold to which a government is obligated to elevate its citizens. Thus, put as simply as possible, my proposal is that the state's institutions must provide each citizen with enough leverage to enable him to acquire further leverage without inordinate difficulty or sacrifice. Expressed with a bit more care, the proposal asserts that the state must provide each citizen with access to some combination of resources and opportunities that makes it possible for him to ascend to increasingly higher levels of resources and opportunities without having to do things that cannot reasonably be expected of him.

In the remainder of the chapter, I will advance an argument which seeks both to clarify the proposed threshold and to show how it is grounded in each person's fundamental interest. However, before I turn to that argument, I want to present a series of examples which are designed to illustrate the difference that an increment of a single size can make to the leverage of agents who begin at different points on the resource/opportunity continuum. My aim in beginning with these examples is both to make the argument that follows easier to grasp and to bring out the intuitive appeal of the proposed threshold.

IV

Because resources and opportunities are interdependent, and because the form of leverage that concerns us is the ability to increase one's combined amount of both, it will not matter whether the comparisons in our examples are couched in terms of resources, of opportunities, or of a combination of each. Thus, to keep things as simple as possible, I will stipulate that the parties in the examples all have exactly the same opportunities but different amounts of money, and I will consider only the effects of a straight subsidy of an additional fifty dollars a week on the leverage of each. My aim in framing the examples in these terms is not to suggest that the best way for the state to bring its citizens up to the leverage threshold *is* to provide them with subsidies – that is not a question I will address – but is only to make the sequence as vivid as possible.

Consider, first, the subsidy's effect on Despera, a wretchedly poor individual whose pre-subsidy income falls exactly fifty dollars a week short of meeting her daily needs. When the state provides Despera with an additional fifty dollars, her only choice is to use it for food or shelter. Because she has no initial leverage, and because she must devote the entire increment to her immediate survival, the subsidy brings Despera neither an absolute nor (therefore) a proportional gain in her leverage.

Consider next the subsidy's effect on Pover, whose income without the extra money is just equivalent to what Despera earns with it. Left to his own devices, Pover earns exactly enough to meet his needs with nothing left over. Thus, when the state provides him with an additional fifty dollars a week, he can use the increment in a number of ways: to purchase a few small luxuries, to provide a margin of safety against future shortfalls, or to put himself in a position to acquire further resources or opportunities (for example, by buying a bicycle or taking a bus to apply for a job that pays a higher wage). Because the extra money opens up the latter possibilities, and because Pover previously had no leverage at all, the subsidy represents both a significant absolute and an infinite proportional increase in Pover's leverage.

Consider next the subsidy's impact on Margina, whose income without the subsidy is just equivalent to what Pover earns with it. Left to her own devices, Margina has an income that exceeds her daily needs by fifty dollars a week. Thus, when the state provides her with the additional fifty dollars, she can again use it in various ways: to increase her discretionary purchases, as an additional hedge against future shortfalls, or as a means to acquiring further resources and opportunities. However, because Margina begins with a modest initial surplus, the attraction of the first two uses is likely to be less urgent to her than it is to Pover, while the gains she can achieve from the third use are likely to be greater. When the new money is combined with what she already has, it will allow her to save more quickly for a down payment on a used car, endure a longer period of unemployment while searching for a better job, or enroll in a night class to improve her skills. Compared to Pover, Margina gains less leverage in proportion to what she already has, but her absolute gain is greater. In addition, because her life already contains a few luxuries, she is likely to find it easier than Pover to take advantage of her new leverage.

To complete the unfolding picture, let us skip ahead a good many steps to Adequus, who earns a solid middle-class income of (say) sixty thousand dollars a year. Though far from rich, Adequus already has enough of a surplus to be able to increase his wealth and range of opportunities in various ways. He can invest modestly in the stock market, relocate to a more prosperous area, take classes to upgrade his skills, and roam the internet to seek out further possibilities. Although the extra fifty dollars brings him only a small increase in leverage relative to what he already has, his absolute increase is greater than those enjoyed by Pover, Margina, and Despera because he can take advantage of opportunities that require larger outlays than they can afford. Also, of course, using the additional fifty dollars to increase his wealth will require far less effort, ingenuity, or sacrifice on his part than it will for Pover or Margina.[6]

Of the individuals just discussed, each with the exception of Despera gains enough leverage from his subsidy to make further advances in leverage easier. Thus, by the proposed criterion, whether the subsidy brings any of them up to the sufficiency threshold will depend on whether any of its recipients can reasonably be expected to do what is needed to achieve significant further gains in leverage. For example, if it is reasonable to expect the post-subsidy Pover to recognize and perform the actions that such an ascent would require, then Pover's subsidy will already bring him above the threshold, and so no one with a higher initial income will need to be subsidized. In that case, whether Pover in fact uses his leverage to gain further resources or opportunities (and thus also further leverage) will properly be left up to him. By contrast, if the requisite degree of resourcefulness and perseverance is *more* than the post-subsidy Pover can reasonably be expected to muster, then Pover's subsidy will not fully meet the demands of justice, and so the state will be obligated to increase his leverage by elevating him to a still higher level of resources or opportunities. For each increase in Pover's subsidy, the question of

---

[6] Because Adequus already has so many advantages, I assume that he falls safely above whatever threshold determines the amounts of income and resources to which governments are obligated to provide their citizens access. I assume, that is, that in his case the subsidy is not a requirement of justice. However, here as above, nothing turns on this assumption. If any reader thinks that justice does require this subsidy, he is welcome to extend the sequence by adding a further character (Plena?) who surpasses even his more generous threshold.

whether it is reasonable to expect him to make the increasingly less demanding efforts that gaining additional leverage requires will arise again, and it will continue to arise until it receives a positive answer.

V

Bearing these examples in mind, let us return to the question of justification. I have suggested that we can move from the premise that each person has a fundamental interest in living his life effectively to the conclusion that each person must have at least the specified amount of leverage. But how, exactly, might the argument run?

This question is best addressed in stages. To answer it, I will have to explain, first, why satisfying a person's fundamental interest in living his life effectively requires bringing him up to *any* resource/opportunity threshold; second, why that threshold must be couched in terms of leverage over resources and opportunities rather than simple amounts of them; third, why, and in what sense, the activities through which an agent would exercise his leverage must be ones he can reasonably be expected to perform; and, fourth, how great a rate of increase in resources and opportunities those activities must allow the agent to achieve. Let me now try to answer these questions in order.

Why, first, should enabling someone to live his life effectively require elevating him above *any* resource or opportunity threshold? This is, in effect, a variant of the question that arose at the end of the previous chapter — namely, "If living effectively requires adjusting one's aspirations to one's limitations, then why can't agents live effectively no matter how limited their resources and opportunities?" — and I won't repeat everything I said in response. Instead, I will reiterate only the most important point, which is that the same deeply entrenched psychology which channels us into reason-guided activity, and thus inclines us to temper our aspirations when this is rationally required, is also a source of various substantive demands which limit the accommodations we can rationally make.

For, to cite just a few obvious examples, all normal humans enjoy pleasure and comfort, are averse to discomfort and pain, and prefer good health to bad, freedom to constraint, and security to insecurity. In addition, we all have unique constellations of tastes, values, and predilections which dispose us to find some pursuits and projects attractive and worthy while others leave us cold. These commonalities may not run as deep as the assumptions about time, space, and reasons that structure our practical thought, but together they give content to the sort of life for which we are suited. This suggests that no one can live his life effectively if his level of resources and opportunities is so low as to deprive him of access to virtually everything that creatures like us find congenial. And as long as we accept any such view – as, surely, we should – we are indeed committed to some kind of resource or opportunity threshold.

But why, next, should that threshold be couched in terms of leverage rather than simple amounts of resources and opportunities? Why not say, more straightforwardly, that what each person needs is a certain number of dollars and a certain bundle of opportunities? As just posed, this question is confused, in that it wrongly suggests that the two ways of specifying the resource/opportunity threshold are competitors. As we have seen, the crucial question about any absolute specification of that threshold is why it should be set at just the specified point and not higher or lower; and the leverage account is best understood as providing an answer to this question. By requiring that each citizen have access to a level of resources and opportunities that enables him not only to enjoy some rudimentary amenities and pursue some personal projects, but also to enlarge his stock of resources and opportunities without having to perform actions that cannot reasonably be expected of him, it seeks to identify the relevant absolute levels in a manner that is principled rather than arbitrary.

There is, moreover, good reason to accept its answer; for no other response fits as well with the broader aim of enabling each person to live his own life effectively. If instead we tried to pin down the absolute resource/opportunity threshold *without* appealing to the amounts of leverage that agents must have, then we would have to do so on the grounds that there is some specific range of goals (activities, outcomes) to which each agent must have access, and that the relevant absolute threshold is whatever level of resources and opportunities *provides* an agent with such access. An argument of this sort would not commit us to any judgments about which goals within the favored range are more worth achieving than which others, but it would commit us to the judgment that access to the goals within that range is morally significant in a way that access to whatever further goals a higher absolute threshold would bring within reach is not. Without further backing – and none appears to be in the offing – any such judgment would simply be arbitrary. In addition, any state which relied on such a judgment would be preempting the judgments of those citizens who would pursue the further goals if given the chance. This way of proceeding would be in tension, if not outright conflict, with the aim of enabling citizens effectively to determine the shape of their own lives.

But we can greatly reduce this tension by making it possible for any citizen who views the range of goals that is associated with his current level of resources and opportunities as too confining to take action to expand that range. By giving people a reasonable chance to increase their stock of resources and opportunities, we also make it reasonable for them to deliberate about the advisability of seeking goals that are currently beyond their reach. This both greatly extends the scope of the activities into which each person's consciousness unavoidably channels him and enables each person to pursue many goals whose suitability to his situation, history, or temperament would otherwise be rendered moot by their unavailability. Although our ability to exercise control over our lives will always be severely limited – one main lesson of the preceding chapter was that we are all adrift in a sea of contingency – we will exercise significantly more control if we can affect our own level of resources and opportunities than if we cannot. And that, surely, is a sufficient justification for specifying the resource/opportunity threshold in terms of the leverage that these goods provide.

VI

This reasoning provides a basic framework for a defense of a leverage threshold; but as presented, it tells us neither how easily a person

with a sufficient amount of leverage must be able to increase his stock
of opportunities and resources nor what rate of increase he must be
able to achieve. Given its silence on these questions, the reasoning
is compatible with a very wide range of absolute thresholds. On the
one hand, because the reasoning imposes no limits on the difficulty
of what an agent must do to exercise his leverage, and because it
does not rule out a very low rate of increase, it is compatible with
an absolute threshold that gives an agent very little to work with –
at the limit, exactly what he needs to survive plus one extra dollar –
and that therefore allows him to make only an agonizingly slow
series of minuscule gains. Conversely, because the reasoning does not
prevent us from requiring that agents be able to achieve a *high* rate of
increase, and to do so with minimal effort, it is also compatible with
an absolute threshold that matches or exceeds the level of provision
of a Scandinavian welfare state. Even allowing for the unavoidable
imprecision of our subject matter, any sufficiency account that did not
rule out one or another of these absolute thresholds would be of little
practical use.

Thus, to sharpen my defense of the leverage approach, I must now
explain how the same considerations that support it in its general form
can also help us make it more precise. As a first step, we must remind
ourselves of two observations that have already been made: first, that
the ability to live one's life effectively requires not merely the ability
to survive from one day to the next, but also a modicum of security
and access to basic comforts, pleasures, and optional activities; and,
second, that each successful use of one's resources or opportunities
to increase one's stock of them tends to make the next increase of
comparable size easier. From the first observation, we may infer that
even the lowest acceptable absolute threshold will extend significantly
beyond what is needed for bare survival, and hence that anyone who
reaches it must already be able to exercise a non-trivial amount of
leverage if he is willing to forgo the comforts, pleasures, or optional
activities that his additional resources and opportunities make possible. Moreover, from the second observation – that a person's leverage
tends to increase as he exercises it – we may draw the additional
inference that such sacrifices may well only be temporary, and that

once the agent has increased his leverage a certain amount by making them, he can expect any further gains to be won at less cost to his personal life.

These considerations suggest that anyone whose level of resources and opportunities is high enough to enable him to enjoy some rudimentary amenities, and who therefore has the option of sacrificing those amenities to gain additional resources and opportunities, is already in a position to step on the up escalator. Thus, if the ability to get onto the escalator were all that mattered, then anyone with any leeway at all would already have reached the leverage threshold. However, in fact, the situation is not this simple; for it is easy to envision situations in which a person's leverage does *not* enhance his ability to live his life effectively. In particular, that ability will not be enhanced if the only way for him to exercise his leverage is to do things that he finds impossible or inordinately difficult, if the magnitude or duration of the sacrifices that he would have to make is too great, or if the likelihood that his efforts or sacrifices will pay off is too small. Not coincidentally, these are just the factors that support the claim that an agent cannot reasonably be expected to exercise his leverage; and it was precisely to rule them out that I stipulated that the actions through which an agent can exercise his leverage must not be ones that it is unreasonable to expect him to perform.

Because the cited factors are all associated with low levels of resources and opportunities, the need to mitigate them exerts upward pressure on the leverage threshold. Given the many conceptual and empirical difficulties that we encounter when we try to balance disparate gains and losses in a person's ability to live effectively, it is obviously impossible to be precise about how far we must raise the threshold. Still, even allowing for this, it remains informative to spell out the reasons why each factor compels us to raise it.

Thus, consider first forms of leverage which require actions that are either impossible or very difficult to perform. It is clearly unreasonable to expect an ordinary person to increase his stock of resources and opportunities either by performing feats of superhuman physical strength or endurance or by drawing on knowledge or skills that he simply does not possess.[7] It is also unreasonable to expect him to do so by working so many hours that he never gets a chance to sleep or doing a job that causes him severe and relentless pain. In each case, the reason we discount the claim that the agent would gain additional resources or opportunities by doing these things is that it has no real bearing on his ability to live effectively. This is clearest when the agent decisively lacks the requisite knowledge, strength, or skill – when there is simply no way in which he could do what is required – but something like it also holds when the required actions are not quite impossible, but do lie right at, or very near, the limits of his physical or mental powers. Because people sometimes do push themselves to the limit, we cannot flatly assert that no agent in this position is capable of exercising his leverage. Still, because such feats are so extremely difficult, they require a strength of will that most people do not possess. Thus, in the great majority of cases, a form of leverage whose exercise requires prodigious feats of strength, endurance, imagination, or perseverance will indeed fail to increase its possessor's ability to live effectively. This means that any government that seeks to effect a real increase in that ability must provide its citizens not only with leverage, but also with access to whatever resources and opportunities they need to (become able to) exercise it.

The second factor that limits what can reasonably be expected of a person – the amount he would have to sacrifice to exercise his leverage – operates differently. Here the question is not whether the agent is able to perform the relevant actions, but rather whether his doing so would itself undermine his ability to live effectively. There are, of course, many sacrifices that do enhance an agent's ability to live effectively, and these are ones he can reasonably be expected to make. However, the situation looks different when a person cannot increase

---

[7] In each of these cases, expecting the agent to perform the relevant actions is unreasonable in both an epistemic sense (since we have good reason to expect that he will not perform them) and the moral sense (since we are being unreasonable if we demand that they be performed). However, in each case, too, it is precisely because we know that something will in fact prevent the agent from performing the actions that we are unreasonable if we demand *that* he perform them.

his stock of resources or opportunities without badly damaging his health or mental abilities, without spending so many years at repetitive, mindless tasks that he will have little time left to use what he gains, or without betraying or compromising the deeply held values to which his deliberations have led him. These are sacrifices that agents often *cannot* reasonably be expected to make, and the natural explanation is precisely that each can undermine their ability to live effectively to a degree that cancels any potential gains. Thus, genuinely to increase that ability, the state must give its citizens access to levels of resources and opportunities that are high enough not only to provide leverage, but also to permit its exercise in ways that do not cancel any projected gains.

The third and final factor that limits what people can reasonably be expected to do to exercise their leverage – the likelihood that their efforts and sacrifices will not pay off – operates differently again. When the only available ways of increasing one's resources or opportunities are very likely to fail, any projected increase in one's ability to live effectively may simply be swamped by the time and energy one would have to expend and the preferable alternatives one would have to forgo. Whatever else is true, persisting in a Quixotic quest is not living one's life effectively. This is, I think, the factor that exerts the strongest upward pressure on the leverage threshold; for when a person has little margin for error, his prospects for success are always precarious. The plans of the working poor are easily defeated by sudden illnesses, layoffs, and many other unexpected misfortunes, and when someone has been unemployed for many years, is illiterate, or has spent much of his life in prison, his prospects of success are obviously bleaker yet. With each increase in the probability of failure, the increase in effectiveness that a successful exercise of leverage would bring is more heavily discounted, while the costs of making the effort remain the same. Thus, to avoid making it unreasonable to expect those at the bottom to try, the state must provide each with access to a package of resources and opportunities that affords him a reasonable chance of succeeding if he *does* try.

One final question remains, and that is what rate of increase an acceptable leverage threshold must make possible. However, this question need not detain us long because its answer is implicit in what has already been said. To be able to achieve a given rate of increase, an agent must be able to gain a certain additional quantity of resources or opportunities within a certain period of time. We have already seen that agents cannot reasonably be expected to exercise their leverage if the eventual gains in effectiveness would be outweighed by the lengthy periods of lessened effectiveness that would have to precede them. These are precisely the cases in which the rate of increase is too low. Thus, to specify the minimally acceptable rate of increase, we can simply identify it with the lowest rate at which this problem does not arise.[8]

VII

In the preceding sections, I have proposed a sufficientarian answer to the question of how the state should distribute resources and opportunities. Moreover, unlike most other sufficientarians, I have tried to defend a particular account of how much is enough. Because all sufficiency accounts are controversial, and because mine in particular has been laid out quickly and schematically, there are bound to be many questions about what I have said. Thus, before I proceed, I want to anticipate and preemptively answer the most predictable objections. These I take to be the objections that my leverage threshold is (1) too low, (2) too high, (3) too rigid, (4) too bourgeois, and (5) too unequal.

1. *Too low?* I have defended my threshold on the grounds that those who can increase their stock of resources and opportunities are better able to live their lives effectively than those who cannot. However, this establishes at most that enabling citizens to live effectively requires elevating them *at least* to the leverage threshold. That leaves open the question of whether they must be elevated further. Moreover, because the ability to live effectively is itself a matter of degree, isn't there a

---

[8] Because I believe that affluent societies do have the resources to bring all their citizens up to the leverage threshold, I have not addressed the question of how they should weigh the interests of citizens who fall short of it by different amounts. However, if this question were to arise, one natural response would be to assign some form of (deontic) priority to those whose shortfall is greatest.

strong case for the view that the resource/opportunity threshold must indeed be higher?

My final response to this objection will be that there is a point at which the ability to live effectively ceases to be a matter of degree, and that to reach that point an agent need ascend no further on the resource/opportunity continuum than the leverage threshold. However, because this response is part of my bottom-up argument, I am not yet in a position to make it here. But neither do I need to make it, since another, more available response will do as well. Put most simply, the further response is that anyone with the requisite amount of leverage is already in a position to ascend to any higher level of resources and opportunities that might plausibly be proposed as an alternative threshold, and that a higher level of initial provision is therefore unnecessary. Although any given agent's attempts to climb the ladder may of course fail, that possibility is no more damaging to the leverage threshold than the equivalent possibility of falling *back* to the leverage threshold is to some higher one. Moreover, in any case, it follows from the reasonable-expectations requirement that any agent whose resources and opportunities reach the leverage threshold will have a good chance of ascending further up the ladder. Taken together, these considerations suggest that any state which elevates each citizen to the leverage threshold (and of course to all other relevant thresholds) has indeed fulfilled its distributive obligations.

2. *Too high?* But is it even *necessary* to elevate each citizen to the leverage threshold as I have described it? Must a just society really make it possible for each citizen to increase his stock of resources and opportunities without sustaining a net loss in his ability to live effectively? Doesn't this requirement conflict with our earlier conclusion that enabling people to live their lives effectively means allowing the predictable consequences of even their poor decisions to play themselves out? And, in a more practical vein, doesn't it call for expenditures that are massive even for affluent societies and that lie well beyond the reach of non-affluent ones?

In each case, I think the answer is "no." To square the no-net-loss requirement with our conclusion that people must be allowed to make and live with their own mistakes, I need only point out that the no-net-loss requirement governs only what agents must be *able* to do, but not what they must *in fact* do. It is perfectly consistent to say both that each agent must have a way of gaining additional resources or opportunities that does not diminish his overall ability to live effectively and that each agent must be free to (try to) increase his resources and opportunities in ways that in fact do diminish that ability. Nor, further, would elevating each citizen to the leverage threshold necessarily be too costly; for there is no direct relation between the amounts of opportunity or resources a society makes available to its citizens and how much it spends in doing so. Here my earlier talk of subsidies must not mislead. A person's opportunities, and so too the resources to which he has access, depend not only on his income and bank account, but also on myriad further factors that include the dynamism of his society's economy, the attitudes of its members toward him and people like him, the incentives and constraints that are built into its culture and any relevant subcultures, the structure of the legal system, and the transportation, education, and information options that the society provides.[9] There is no reason to expect that combinations of these factors which provide all members of society with suitable levels of opportunity and access to resources will be more costly than ones that do not. Thus, because our ability to manipulate our social arrangements is limited only by our ingenuity and our political will, the cost of bringing each citizen up to the leverage threshold is at worst radically indeterminate.

3. *Too rigid?* So far, I have spoken as though there is some single absolute level of resources and opportunities that provides each citizen with a sufficient amount of leverage. But is this one-size-fits-all assumption really consistent with my claim that each person must be able to exercise his leverage without having to do anything that

---

[9] Amartya Sen and Martha Nussbaum have both written extensively about the ways in which social and institutional arrangements affect the opportunities of those who live under them. Two relevant representative works are Amartya Sen, *Development as Freedom* (New York: Anchor Books, 1999), and Martha Nussbaum, *Women and Human Development: The Capabilities Approach* (Cambridge University Press, 2000). For a useful bibliography of further work by both authors, see Nussbaum, *Creating Capabilities*.

cannot reasonably be expected of him? Can't two people with the same resources and opportunities have differing value-commitments which make it unreasonable to expect one, but not the other, to exercise his leverage? Don't differences in talent also make it reasonable to expect more from some than from others? And, hence, mustn't we abandon the idea that there is some single amount of resources and opportunities that provides each person with sufficient leverage, and replace it with a far less rigid and more individualized account of the absolute threshold?

The answer, I think, is that there is indeed some play in what can reasonably be expected of people, but that this does not defeat the claim that a society can bring (almost) all of its members up to the leverage threshold by providing each with access to the same absolute amounts of resources and opportunities. It is of course true that when two people with the same resources and opportunities have different value-commitments, the first will often have a reason to exercise his leverage that the second lacks. However, even in cases like this, the second person's value-commitments are unlikely to *rule out* (as opposed to merely not requiring) the relevant efforts and sacrifices; and as long as this is true, these kinds of efforts and sacrifices will still be ones that both parties can reasonably be expected to make. It is also true that we cannot reasonably expect persons with very different levels of talent to accomplish the same amounts; but here the way to avoid the need for different absolute thresholds is simply to relativize our notion of what can reasonably be expected of a person to the average range of talents within which the great majority of individuals fall. Although this will not bring the leverage threshold within reach of those whose talents are markedly *below* average, there is something like a consensus that such persons require some form of special treatment, and that is a consensus I am glad to join.

4. *Too bourgeois?* To exercise leverage over his resources and opportunities, a person must be prudent, calculating, and willing to defer gratification. These traits define the much-maligned bourgeois sensibility, and some may therefore object that the leverage threshold reflects a cramped and unworthy vision of human possibilities. I believe, in fact, that the bourgeois virtues are the bedrock of civilized

life and that they are as compatible with altruistic as with selfish aims, but I need not defend these claims here. Instead, what matters for present purposes is simply that prudence is the virtue that matches the goods whose distribution is currently under discussion. Resources and opportunities exist only to be used, and whatever considerations give us reason to use them at all must also give us reason to try to acquire as much of them as we have reason *to* use. It therefore should come as no surprise that the principle that determines when an agent has enough of these goods is one that makes essential reference to the conditions under which he can acquire more.

5. *Too unequal?* How much a person can gain by exercising his leverage depends on where on the resource/opportunity continuum he begins. With some luck and a bit of ingenuity, the post-subsidy Pover may in a few years reach the level that Adequus currently occupies; but if in that time Adequus has the same luck and exercises the same amount of ingenuity, he is likely to gain significantly more. Although each person above the leverage threshold has a spread of probabilities of reaching each higher level within a certain range, both the magnitude of that range and its highest point increase with each increment in one's initial location. Thus, by requiring only that no one fall below the leverage threshold, I am in effect endorsing a system in which some will inevitably have many more options than others.

Because any sufficientarian approach to the distribution of resources and opportunities will have some such inegalitarian implications, one way to deal with this objection is simply to restate the basic case for sufficiency. This I take to be the argument that because individuals matter one by one, it follows that "[w]ith respect to the distribution of economic assets, what *is* important from the point of view of morality is not that everyone should have *the same* but that each should have *enough*."[10] But given the larger account within which the leverage threshold is embedded, I can do better. To those who remain convinced that what matters is not just how much each individual has but also the relations among what different individuals have, I can

[10] Harry Frankfurt, "Equality as a Moral Ideal," in his *The Importance of What We Care About*, p. 134; italics in original.

respond that at a more basic distributive level – the one that concerns not just instrumentalities but the ability to use them effectively – I too am committed to equality. The reasoning behind this claim, which I have already anticipated, is that the state must seek to elevate each citizen's ability to live effectively to the highest level that he can reach, and that any state that does this will equally satisfy each person's fundamental interest. To flesh this reasoning out, I will have to provide the bottom-up argument that I promised at the beginning of the chapter; and that, accordingly, is my next task.

CHAPTER 9

From sufficiency to equality

In this, the book's final chapter, I will directly confront the question of where to set the effectiveness threshold. Reduced to its essentials, my argument will be, first, that the state is obligated to render each citizen as able to live effectively as he can be, but, second, that to get to this maximum, a citizen need only reach the leverage threshold and the other complementary thresholds that were defended in the previous chapter. By assigning this new role to these familiar thresholds, I will attempt both to establish the convergence of the top-down and bottom-up approaches and to complete the transition from a sufficientarian to an egalitarian account. Then, to round out the discussion, I will return to the main unanswered questions about how a person's choices should affect his fortunes at the different stages of his life.

I

To live our lives effectively, I have argued, is to satisfy the standards that are internal to the activities into which our consciousness channels us. Satisfying these standards involves embracing ends that we in fact have reason to pursue, conceiving and adopting plans that are well suited to accomplish those ends, and executing the plans in ways that are efficient and flexible. Because a person can be more or less proficient at each activity, the ability to live effectively, to which each contributes, must also come in degrees. Thus, the question we must now ask is "To what level of that overall ability is the state obligated to elevate its citizens?"

The task of answering this question is complicated by the absence of an obvious upper limit to the ability to deliberate or plan or execute one's plans. No matter how much a person knows about himself and his circumstances, and no matter how well he appreciates the ends that his situation gives him reason to pursue, it is always possible to know more and to have a more refined sense of the situation's normative relevance. No matter how resourceful a person is at thinking up ingenious ways of accomplishing disparate ends, it is always possible to be more resourceful yet. No matter how adept and flexible a person is at implementing his plans, and no matter how many resources and opportunities he has at his disposal, it is always possible to be even more adept and to have even more resources. And because a person's overall ability to live effectively depends on how well he can perform each of these more specific activities, their having no upper limits may appear to support the conclusion that the overall ability has no upper limit either.

If this inference were correct, then the level of ability to live effectively to which the state must elevate its citizens would have to occupy some intermediate point on the effectiveness continuum. That would raise the familiar question of why the threshold should be set at just that point and not some higher or lower one – a question that I, at least, would not know how to answer. However, in what follows, I will argue that the inference fails, and that the ability to live effectively does have an upper limit. I will argue, as well, that that upper limit *just is* the threshold of effectiveness to which the state must elevate its citizens.

In saying this, I do not mean to suggest that each person's ability to live effectively has the *same* upper limit. To the contrary, because people differ greatly in judgment and reasoning ability, and because governmental efforts to eliminate these differences are neither permissible nor likely to succeed, I expect that the highest levels of overall effectiveness that different people can attain will vary dramatically. But even if they do, each person's upper limit will remain the most salient point, both psychologically and morally, on the continuum of levels of ability to live effectively that he might reach. Thus, if we can establish both that each person has such an upper limit and that elevating him to it is something his government can do, then our question of where to locate the effectiveness threshold will have a natural and satisfying answer.

II

But *can* we establish either thing? Why, exactly, should we suppose that there is any point beyond which the acquisition of further resources, further opportunities, or further education would bring no further increase in a person's ability to live effectively? And why, if there is such a point, should we suppose that the amounts of resources, opportunities, and education that it requires are ones to which the state can provide all citizens with access? To see how to answer these questions, and thus how to flesh out the bottom-up argument, we must first review the factors that limit people's proficiency at deliberating and planning and executing their plans.

Of those factors, some are aspects of the agent's own constitution while others are aspects of his external situation. At the deliberative stage, he may be rendered less able to recognize what is truly choice-worthy by his lack of imagination, his ignorance of some crucial fact, the shoddiness of his reasoning, or his lack of insight into his own attitudes or aptitudes. At the planning stage, he may be prevented from finding a way to achieve his ends by any of these factors, but also by the inadequacy of his resources or opportunities, his lack of access to some necessary technology, or his inability to coordinate with others or win their cooperation. At the execution stage, his way forward may again be blocked by any of the foregoing factors, but also by any number of unforeseen events to which he cannot successfully adapt or adjust. Although each such limitation is in principle causally explicable, and although many are within the control either of other individuals or of the wider society, none is within the immediate control of the agent himself. Insofar as he is aware of them at all, the limiting factors must all present themselves to him as brute contingencies.

But if so, then they must themselves be among the contingencies that provide the context within which the agent must make a life. No less than his good or bad health, his predilections and aversions, or the vicissitudes of his marriage, the factors that limit a person's ability to deliberate or plan or execute his plans are all aspects of the overall situation to which his deliberation and planning and execution are responses. And just as someone can bring to consciousness, and can alter his plans in light of, such factors as a delay in his timetable or an unexpected shortage of funds, so too can he adjust to his own tendency to be overly optimistic or his lack of talent at an activity he loves. This opens up the possibility that the factors that limit someone's effectiveness may themselves be among the contingencies with which he can deal effectively.

The idea that a person might deploy his imperfect abilities in the service of reducing their imperfections – that he might deliberate, plan, and act in ways that enable him to overcome the deficits that render him less effective than he might otherwise be *at* deliberating or planning or implementing his plans – is an obvious extension of the idea that he can deploy his limited resources or opportunities in the service of gaining more of them. However, unlike the claim that we can exercise leverage over our resources and opportunities, the claim that we can bootstrap our way to improvements in the other components of effectiveness has an air of paradox about it. For if someone is unaware of the factors that determine what he has most reason to seek, then won't he also be unaware of the need to acquire the information he lacks? If someone is too muddled to form a coherent plan, won't he also be too muddled to seek greater clarity? If someone is too impulsive to stick with his plans, won't he also be too impulsive to stick with a plan to reduce his impulsiveness?

There is obviously something to this objection, but the point must not be overstated. To appreciate its limitations, we need only remind ourselves of the different ways in which the generalization upon which it rests – namely, that any impediment to an agent's effectiveness will also also impede its own elimination – can fail. There are, broadly speaking, three such ways. For one thing, the impediment may be only partial, as when a person who lacks enough information to form an effective plan does have enough information to know just what further information he needs, or when a person with bad judgment has good enough judgment to recognize the need for improvement. For another, the agent may be able to mitigate the impediment by exercising abilities that it does not impede, as when a person who is held back by a lack of education takes advantage of an opportunity to acquire one or when someone who is hopeless at math gets help with his taxes. Moreover, third, even if the same factor that prevents a person from living his life effectively also does prevent him from removing the impediment, it need not have the same effect on others. Even if I have too little education to recognize the need for more education, or am too undisciplined to take steps to become more disciplined, it is often possible for my friends, my family, or the state to do what I cannot.

Because the first two possibilities exist, each agent is often in a position to gain a purchase on the factors that reduce his effectiveness; while because the third possibility exists, the state is often in a position to put agents in this position if they are not there to begin with. Moreover, with each increase in a person's education, judgment, reasoning ability, resources, and level of opportunity, there are fewer impediments to successful deliberation, planning, and execution that he must overcome and more potential ways of overcoming them. This suggests that there may be some combined level of education, resources, and the rest which is high enough to enable a person to overcome *any and all* of the impediments to successful deliberation, planning, and execution that his remaining deficiencies in these areas impose. If this conjecture is correct, then someone who reaches this level will be as able to live his life effectively as anyone can be, and so the ability to live effectively will indeed have an upper limit.

Should we accept the conjecture? Against it, someone might object that because there is no upper limit to how expensive it can be to accomplish a person's rational aims, there is also no upper limit to the amounts of money (opportunity, education) that a fully effective life would require. However, in response, we need only recall that what qualifies as a rational aim for a person is itself a function of the resources and education and opportunities that are available to him, and that, once a high enough level of these goods is reached, the rational way for an agent to respond to any remaining shortfalls is simply to scale back his aims. This of course will not render the agent maximally able to live effectively unless he can recognize and respond to all the reasons that his situation provides; but for theoretical purposes, we can simply follow the economists by stipulating that we are dealing only with agents who are fully rational. Because this stipulation seems coherent, I am inclined to believe the ability to live effectively does have a theoretical upper limit.

Yet even if it does, that limit will not be one to which the state can actually elevate its citizens. The main problem here is not that a government may not be able to provide all citizens with access to the relevant amounts of resources, opportunity, and education, but is rather that it definitely cannot elevate them all to the requisite levels of judgment and reasoning. There are well-known empirical limits to human rationality,[1] and even within these boundaries, people's rational capacities vary widely. There is no known way of making foolish people wise, and as we saw in Chapter 7, any governmental attempts to do so would in any case be unacceptably intrusive. Because bad judgment and poor habits of reasoning are both widespread and intractable, many will always lack the wit to take advantage of even the highest levels of resources and opportunities and education. Even with all the help in the world, these individuals will never be able to overcome the internal shortcomings that prevent them from deliberating or planning or executing as well as others.

Yet even if no one can possibly reach the theoretical upper limit of effectiveness, there is, for each person, a *lower* upper limit of effectiveness that *is* within his reach. To bring this out, we need only ask how a person who has reached the limits of his capacities to reason and judge is likely to fare as his levels of resources, opportunity, and education continue to rise. The answer, pretty clearly, is that as those levels increase, their incremental impact on the agent's ability to compensate for his deliberative and executive shortcomings will gradually decrease. There are only so many strategies for blunting

---

[1] The literature on this subject is voluminous. Many important papers are collected in Daniel Kahneman, Paul Slovik, and Amos Tversky, eds., *Judgment under Uncertainty: Heuristics and Biases* (Cambridge University Press, 1982).

the impact of one's bad judgment or inability to think clearly, and most of these (seeking advice, buying a day planner, reading self-help books) neither cost very much nor require much in the way of opportunity or education. Thus, as the agent's resources, opportunities, and education continue to increase, he will rather quickly reach a point at which the only thing stopping him from overcoming the remaining obstacles to effectiveness is his own inability to use what he already has. When someone reaches this point, no additional infusion of these goods will bring any further increase in his ability to overcome his cognitive and judgmental shortcomings. Thus, even if such a person remains far less able to recognize and respond to his reasons than others, he will at least have reached the highest level of effectiveness that is available to him.

III

But it is one thing to make the case that each person's ability to live effectively tops out at a certain point, and quite another to show that any government is obligated to elevate each citizen *to* his theoretical maximum. The issue here is not whether the state must bring each citizen up to *some* threshold of effectiveness – I have already defended this claim on the grounds that the state is obligated to advance each citizen's fundamental interest in living his life effectively – but instead is whether the upper limit of each person's ability to live effectively is the *appropriate* threshold. That it is is suggested both by that upper limit's moral salience and by the fact that elevating someone to it would leave him with no room for complaint. However, before we can accept this suggestion, we will have to get clearer about the levels of resources and other subordinate goods that a person must have to *reach* his upper limit; and we will also have to ask whether access to these levels is something his government can reasonably be expected to provide.

The first question – what level of each subordinate good does a person need to be able to compensate for his remaining deficits in each area? – has no single answer; for as someone's level of any one good rises, he becomes able to compensate for increasingly serious deficits in others. Someone who is exceptionally well educated may see opportunities that others don't, while those with rich parents can get past missteps that would ruin someone of more modest means. However, these extremes are unhelpful because only the academically gifted can reach the highest levels of education and no government can make all of its citizens exceptionally rich. Thus, for our purposes, the relevant levels are ones that are all low enough to be within a government's power to make available to all. And, predictably enough, the levels I think are most eligible are precisely those I defended on independent grounds in the preceding chapter.

Let me briefly recap what I said there. There are, I suggested, at least three independently defensible subordinate thresholds, one governing combinations of resources and opportunities, another governing education, and a third governing judgment and reasoning ability. Where resources and opportunities are concerned, the crucial level is the leverage threshold — that is, the level at which an agent can ascend to increasingly higher levels of resources and opportunities without having to do things that cannot reasonably be expected of him. Where education is concerned, it is whatever combination of knowledge and skills enables a person to recognize the main facts about his situation that give him reason to seek some ends rather than others and to deploy his resources and opportunities in some ways rather than others. Where reasoning and judgment (and, we may add, imagination) are concerned, it is, for each person, the level of competence that he will reach in the natural course of things if he is raised in moderately fortunate circumstances.

To see why elevating someone to this combination of thresholds will bring him right up to the limit of his ability to live effectively, we need only consider the thresholds one by one. The reasoning and judgment threshold has been set where it is because the state cannot do much to improve these abilities once someone is an adult; and this already rules out the possibility of increasing someone's ability to live effectively by elevating him *above* that threshold. Nor, for different reasons, can the state increase anyone's ability to live effectively by elevating him above the *education* threshold; for by specifying that threshold in terms of what people must know in order to recognize and respond to the main reason-giving aspects of their situations, we have already established both that its substantive requirements will be adequate to their situations and that those requirements will evolve as new forms of knowledge and skill become necessary.[2] Moreover, because a person's situation often gives him reason to engage in activities which will *extend* the range of reasons to which he has the knowledge and skills to respond – activities such as availing himself of educational opportunities, investigating crucial aspects of his situation, and reflecting on his limitations – providing each person with the knowledge he needs to recognize his reasons will also insure that each person knows enough to remedy his own deficiencies in these areas.

Thus, if any subsidiary threshold is to leave room for the possibility that someone might become able to live even more effectively by surpassing it, it will have to be the leverage threshold. The claim will have to be that Margina, who (we may suppose) sits just at the leverage threshold, remains less able to live her life effectively than Adequus, who surpasses it by a considerable margin. But why, exactly, should this be so? It is true that because Margina begins with less, the upper limit of the range of increases in wealth and opportunity that she can achieve by exercising her leverage is lower than the upper limit of the range that Adequus can achieve by exercising his. However, because the ends that any given person has reason to seek are in part a function of what that person can reasonably hope to accomplish, it is also true that Margina's inability to reach the level of wealth that is available to Adequus will itself give her reason to seek more modest ends. For this reason, her rational ends will not be any less accessible to her than

---

[2] An obvious complication here is that, as society and technology become more complex, the forms of knowledge and skill that they require may come to exceed the intellectual capacities of increasing numbers of citizens. Because a person's intellectual capacities are no more tractable than his judgment, this complication lends further support to the idea that different people's abilities to live effectively have different upper limits. However, because the social conditions that require increasingly complex forms of skill and knowledge are tractable in a way that the need for good judgment is not, the complication also suggests that societies have reason to minimize the degree to which the ability to live effectively requires knowledge and skills that are not within the reach of all.

Adequus's are to him. And, hence, if Margina's lower starting point is to render her less able to live effectively than she might otherwise be, the reason can only be that having more resources or opportunities would increase her ability to overcome one or another obstacle to her *achieving* some otherwise accessible rational aim.

But which obstacle might that be? It cannot simply be the obstacle of *having* limited resources and opportunities, since this has already been accommodated through the adjustment of her rational aims and plans to what she has. It also cannot be the obstacle of not knowing enough to recognize what she has reason to do, since anyone who reaches the education threshold either already knows enough to recognize this or else knows what further knowledge or skill he needs to achieve such recognition. There is of course a difference between knowing what further knowledge one needs and having the resources and opportunities to acquire it; but if someone lacks these resources or opportunities (and cannot reasonably hope to obtain them even by exercising his leverage), then the ends that require that amount of knowledge or skill cannot be among the ones that he has reason to pursue. Thus, as long as Margina has reached the leverage and education thresholds, the only obstacles that having more resources or opportunities might render her more able to overcome will be ones that are posed by her flawed judgment or reasoning ability.

As I have repeatedly stressed, I take each person's patterns of judgment to be rooted in deep facts about his character and mental organization, and I therefore view global defects of judgment as highly resistant to change. For this reason, I think it very doubtful that providing individuals with resources or opportunities that exceed the leverage threshold will significantly improve their chances of overcoming the obstacles to effectiveness that their bad judgment poses. This is not to deny that persons with specific defects of judgment – someone with a history of self-defeating choices, for example, or someone who repeatedly gravitates toward abusive partners – may benefit greatly from therapy. However, where such local defects are concerned, the cost of intervention seems unlikely to exceed what someone like Margina can acquire by exercising her leverage. Moreover, even if this supposition is incorrect, it will remain possible to accommodate the difficulty without abandoning the leverage threshold by simply including the opportunity to acquire the needed form(s) of treatment in the package of opportunities and resources that *provides* the leverage. This move, though inelegant, would represent no major theoretical departure, and would allow us to sidestep the final objection to the claim that anyone who reaches all three subsidiary thresholds is thereby rendered as able to live his life effectively as he can be.

IV

With this conclusion, my discussion of the effectiveness threshold is complete. However, two tasks remain. First, because this and the previous chapter have unfolded in stages, I want to provide a brief overview of their overall structure, and of the view that has emerged. Then, to end, I want to return to the question with which the book began.

When I defended the leverage threshold in Chapter 8, I relied on the premise that we all have a fundamental interest in being able to live our lives effectively, but I assumed nothing about *how* effectively anyone must be able to live. Because my argument there presupposed no particular threshold of effectiveness, I begged no questions by going on to equate the effectiveness threshold with whatever level of effectiveness a person attains by reaching the leverage threshold and the other subordinate thresholds. Because this reasoning takes the less basic subordinate thresholds to determine the location of the more basic effectiveness threshold, it moves in the direction I have called top-down. By contrast, in the current chapter, I began by arguing that the state is obligated to elevate each citizen to an independently specifiable level of effectiveness – namely, the highest he is capable of attaining – and I then went on to defend elevating citizens to each subordinate threshold, including the leverage threshold, as the best way for the state to *discharge* that obligation. This reasoning takes the more basic effectiveness threshold to dictate the locations of the less basic subordinate thresholds, and so moves in the direction I have called bottom-up. Because these top-down and bottom-up arguments have radically different starting points yet converge on the same thresholds, each lends additional support to the other.

Yet precisely because what the two arguments converge on *are* thresholds, it may be wondered whether their conclusions are egalitarian in any important sense. This is, in one respect, a side issue, since what really matters is not how my account is classified but only the cogency of what it says. Still, I do think my distributive account has a significant egalitarian dimension that fits nicely with what has been said about the basis of our moral equality, and I want briefly to bring this out.

As I remarked earlier, the claim that my account is egalitarian would be unproblematic if I held both that the state is obligated to elevate each citizen to the highest level of effectiveness that he can reach and that each person's upper limit of effectiveness is the same. Taken together, those claims would imply that a just society is one in which all citizens have equal amounts of the good of being able to live effectively. However, in fact, I have argued that different individuals have different upper limits of effectiveness; and when this claim is conjoined with the requirement that each citizen be elevated to his upper limit, it yields the very different conclusion that a just society is one whose citizens *differ* in their ability to live effectively. Thus, far from committing me to any form of equality, my version of the sufficiency view may at first seem hopelessly inegalitarian.

But this objection is less decisive than it appears, and to see why, we need only recall what was said earlier about the good of nutrition. As we saw in Chapter 6, if we identify food as a good simply on the grounds that it provides us with calories, then it will follow that those who consume 2,500 calories a day always have less of the good than those who consume 5,000. By contrast, if we say, with greater precision, that the reason food is a good is that its calories provide us with the energy we need to live, then Aristotle's wrestler, Milo, who needs and consumes 5,000 calories a day, will have no more of the good than a sedentary clerk who needs and consumes 2,500. That is clearly what we ought to say; and while the point is less obvious, I think we can say something similar about the good of being able to live effectively.

For just as certain levels of calorie consumption would benefit some people but not others, so too would living certain types of lives. For any given agent, there are many potential lives that require a particular cast of mind or habit of thought – for example, a tendency to notice details, a high level of aggression, or a singleness of purpose – that that agent simply does not possess. Also, of course, many other lives will be ruled out by the limits of his athletic, musical, and intellectual talents. Although an agent may regret his inability to succeed at such a life, a limitation that is so deeply rooted in his own nature is hardly a misfortune (much less a tragedy) for him. Instead, given the mismatch between the way he is and the way he would have to be to succeed, the right thing to say is simply that that is not a life that could be his.[3] And neither, for similar reasons, is it a misfortune to be unable to succeed at a life that requires a level of *judgment or reasoning ability* that surpasses one's upper limit; for here again, what makes such a life inaccessible is precisely the agent's own entrenched mental make-up.

To accommodate this complication, we must refine our understanding of what makes the ability to live effectively a good. Properly understood, what accounts for this is not that that ability increases one's likelihood of success at *any and all* possible continuations of his current life, but only that it increases his likelihood of success at any of the continuing lives *that could be his*. However, as so amended, my account no longer implies that when two people with unequal upper limits of ability to live effectively are both brought to their upper limits, the one with the higher upper is provided with more of the relevant good. Instead, as long as each individual *has* reached his personal upper limit, and so is fully able to live any life that could be his, each agent will indeed have the same amount of the relevant good. And because I have identified the sufficiency threshold for each agent *with* his upper limit, the upshot of this refinement is precisely

---

[3] Compare Jeff McMahan: "To determine whether a person is fortunate or unfortunate, we should compare his condition to the range of conditions that would be realistically possible for him given the highest psychological capacities he has so far achieved or that he has had the intrinsic potential to achieve thus far": Jeff McMahan, *The Ethics of Killing: Problems at the Margins of Life* (Oxford University Press, 2002), p. 153.

to reinstate a version of the claim that my distributive account is egalitarian.[4]

V

But what, finally, does that account tell us about when people should and should not have to suffer the effects of their bad choices? This is a question that I raised, but set aside, near the beginning of my discussion, and I want to end by returning to it.

What makes the question difficult is that it compels us to reconcile two considerations that legitimately pull us in opposing directions. On the one hand, because we are not living our lives effectively unless our decisions have a real impact on our fate, the claim that each person has a fundamental interest in living effectively commits us to the view that even the effects of foolish choices must be often allowed to stick. On the other hand, because each life is lived over time, we cannot simply write off the (often substantial) portion of a person's life that *follows* an especially foolish or unfortunate choice. The challenge is to find a theoretically satisfying way of accommodating both pressures.

There has, in the literature on both equality and sufficiency, been some discussion of whether the demands of these principles apply only to whole lives or also or instead to stretches within them. There has also been discussion of whether earlier deviations from equality or sufficiency can or should subsequently be offset.[5] Because these

---

[4] In his essay "Equality or Priority?" (in Matthew Clayton and Andrew Williams, eds., *The Idea of Equality* [Basingstoke: Palgrave Macmillan, 2000], pp. 81–125), Derek Parfit distinguishes between relational egalitarians, who maintain "that inequality is, in itself, either bad or unjust" (p. 106) and non-relational egalitarians, who accept principles such as the priority view which merely have "a built-in bias toward equality" (*ibid.*). Within this typology, mine is clearly not a relational view because it doesn't say that there's anything at all inherently wrong or bad about one person having more of any good than another. However, unlike other non-relational views, mine has more than a bias toward equality; for it asserts that everyone who reaches the effectiveness threshold *definitely will* occupy the same relative position on the continuum of levels of effectiveness that he could achieve.

[5] For discussion of these issues as they pertain to equality, see Dennis McKerlie, "Equality and Time," *Ethics* 99 (1989): 475–91; for discussion of them as they pertain to sufficiency, see Paula Casal, "Why Sufficiency Is Not Enough," *Ethics* 117 (2007): 314–15.

discussions take seriously the fluctuations in the amounts of goods that individuals have at different points in their lives, they may seem relevant to our concerns. However, the discussants generally proceed on the assumption that the different stages of a person's life are all of equal normative significance, and, in making this assumption, they ignore the normative asymmetries that are introduced by choice. Because they do not even register the possible significance of choice, their conclusions make little contact with the question that interests us.

Does my own view's blend of sufficiency and equality give us a better purchase on that question? Because I take the good whose distribution is most fundamentally in question to involve an ability to make choices that stick, my account does give us reason to assign more weight to advantages or disadvantages that stem from earlier choices than to ones that do not. However, it is one thing to tell us this much, and quite another to tell us when the importance of allowing people's choices to play themselves out is great enough to outweigh that of enabling them to live effectively going forward. The notion of effectiveness, as I have introduced it, simply does not have enough internal structure to support such conclusions. Thus, if the only way to invoke my account were to derive the relevant weightings from its notion of effectiveness, then our question would remain unanswered.

But there is a better way of invoking the account, and that is to look first to the subordinate thresholds that collectively *constitute* the effectiveness threshold. This approach offers several important advantages, the first of which is a quick test for which self-inflicted harms are candidates for mitigation. The key facts here are, first, that every self-inflicted harm involves either the loss of a good or, in the case of suffering, an increase in its negative correlate, and, second, that a self-inflicted harm will only reduce an agent's future effectiveness if it leaves him below the corresponding subordinate threshold. These facts immediately allow us to narrow the field because goods such as pleasure and happiness and the absence of their negative correlates are conspicuously not *governed* by subordinate thresholds. Although many self-inflicted harms consist precisely of pain and suffering, and although many others are accompanied by grief and recriminations, these negative subjective states do not often impair an agent's longer-term ability to live his life effectively.[6] And, for this reason, the state is rarely obligated to mitigate self-inflicted losses of welfare (although it may of course still have humanitarian reasons to do so).

A second important advantage that we gain by focusing on the subordinate thresholds is that although each such threshold does govern the distribution of a good that makes a genuine contribution to a person's ability to live effectively, the question of whether to rescue those whose foolish acts bring them below the threshold does not arise in every case. It does not arise about education, for example, because this good, once acquired, cannot be lost. Conversely, although the upper limits of someone's ability to judge and reason well manifestly *can* be reduced by alcohol or drug overuse, these losses are generally irreversible once they occur. By contrast, there are many self-inflicted losses of resources and opportunities that the state obviously can reverse, and there are many losses of health or functionality that can be corrected through a suitable outlay of funds. Thus, when we look past the lush variety of harms that people inflict on themselves, we find that it is really only resources and opportunities that raise the question that interests us.

And here our focus on the subordinate thresholds offers yet a third advantage; for it suggests a natural way of specifying which self-inflicted losses of resources or opportunities are problematic. On the account I have proposed, a just distribution of resources and opportunities is one in which each citizen is at or above the leverage threshold. Thus, as long as someone does not fall below that threshold, whatever resources or opportunities he gains or loses through his legitimate activities will remain consistent with justice. In cases of this sort, the state will have no role in the affair. Moreover, the great majority of foolish choices do *not* appear to bring agents below the leverage threshold. And, in view of this, my account has the satisfying

---

[6] There are of course exceptions to this generalization, the most obvious of which is chronic debilitating pain.

implication that most of the bad economic effects of people's choices can simply be left to play themselves out.

But what, finally, should we say about the crucial subset of foolish choices that *do* bring agents below the leverage threshold? As we have seen, the case against systematically protecting agents from the effects of their bad choices is that swaddling them in this way prevents them from living lives that are genuinely their own, and thus *a fortiori* from living effectively. However, it is one thing to say that agents cannot live effectively unless they are allowed to suffer the consequences of their bad choices, and quite another to say that they cannot do so unless those consequences are sufficiently dire. At least offhand, there is no obvious reason to tie the ability to live one's life effectively to any particular schedule of rewards and penalties. More specifically, there is no obvious reason why agents should not be able to live effectively in societies in which even the worst available choices will not have consequences that bring them below the leverage threshold. If a society's rewards and penalties are structured in this way, then the course of each person's life will still be determined by the interaction of his choices with an indifferently cooperative world, and his poor choices or bad luck will still often defeat his cherished goals, but the later parts of his life will never be ruined by his earlier bad choices. Under these conditions, there will simply be no conflict between the distributions that justice requires at earlier and later times.

This possibility would be of little moment if the amounts of resources and opportunities that different types of action cause agents to gain or lose were natural and fixed. However, as many have noted, the impact of any given decision on an agent's levels of these goods, and so too on his leverage, is *not* a natural fact, but rather depends on his society's institutions. When someone makes a foolish choice, the degree to which it diminishes his subsequent leverage may depend on such factors as the ease or difficulty with which someone in his position can emerge from bankruptcy, the sorts of barriers that ex-criminals like him face, his prospects for acquiring the medical treatment that would heal his self-inflicted injuries, or the amounts that near-destitute individuals can earn going forward. Of these factors, each is itself a function of his society's legal, social, and economic system, and each element of that system is subject to indefinitely many variations.[7]

And, in view of this, the idea of a society whose members cannot fall below the leverage threshold is far more than a bare logical possibility. With sufficient ingenuity, a moderately affluent society may well be able to maintain institutions whose collective effect is to put even those who have dug themselves into the deepest holes in a position to climb out by themselves. This seems, at any rate, to be no more challenging than maintaining institutions that meet people's needs in ways that bypass their agency. However, if anything like it is possible, then the answer to our final question will fall into place. The obvious way to sidestep the difficulty of reconciling the conflicting requirements of effectiveness at earlier and later moments is simply to adopt arrangements under which those requirements do not conflict.[8]

VI

This breezy answer obviously raises many hard new questions of institutional design. However, those questions lie far beyond my competence, and I have nothing useful to say about them. Thus, to end, I will merely restate the two main normative ideas that have led me to the theoretical position at which I've arrived.

[7] Many philosophers have discussed the considerations that ought to determine the rewards and penalties that attach to different choices. For two discussions that relate directly to the requirement that people's choices be allowed to play themselves out, see Elizabeth Anderson, "How Should Egalitarians Cope with Market Risks?," *Theoretical Inquiries in Law* 9 (2008): 239–70, and Marc Fleurbaey, "Egalitarian Opportunities," *Law and Philosophy* 20 (2001): 499–530.

[8] By thus urging the adoption of institutions that permit no one to fall below the leverage threshold, but that allow pure procedural justice to prevail above it, I am assigning the leverage threshold a role that matches the one that Rawls assigns to the difference principle. However, the difference principle, which sets the Rawlsian baseline, is comparative in the sense that it governs the fortunes of a worst-off group that can only be identified by comparison with other, better-off groups. By contrast, my own version of the baseline is non-comparative; for the leverage threshold applies to individuals one by one, and it takes the acceptable minimum to be determined only by what each person himself is able to do with what he has.

I take as my starting point a strong form of moral individualism which locates each person's fundamental interest exclusively in the success of his own life. This form of individualism leaves ample leeway for further interests that are not self-serving. It can accommodate both the commonsense idea that some or all of us have important interests which encompass the well-being of others and the views of those philosophers who maintain that each person has a generalized interest in not being dominated by others and in living under principles that all could accept. However, because I regard the latter interests as derivative, I think it is a mistake to build a theory of justice on them. Because the primal fact about us is that we are physically and psychologically distinct individuals, I believe that any adequate account of the fundamental interests that justice subserves will have to reflect that fact.

The second main idea that informs my account is that a person's social and economic circumstances are continuous with the innumerable other contingencies that frame his choice situation. From an agent's perspective, his bank balance and job prospects are simply two of the innumerable brute facts that he must cope with in the course of living his life. It is true that money and opportunity can easily dominate someone's thinking when he has too little of them; but under other circumstances, the same is true of family difficulties, ill health, personal limitations, and much else. What really sets wealth and opportunity apart from the other contingencies with which an agent must cope is that their distribution depends to a greater extent on his society's institutional arrangements, and so is much easier for that society to control. However, to whatever extent this difference explains why theorists have focused on resources and opportunities rather than the more fundamental ability to which they contribute, it represents one last illustration of the way in which our preoccupation with control can distort our thinking.

Bibliography

Ackerman, Bruce. *Social Justice and the Liberal State*. New Haven: Yale University Press, 1980.

Anderson, Elizabeth. "What Is the Point of Equality?," *Ethics* 109 (1999): 287–337.

"How Should Egalitarians Cope with Market Risks?," *Theoretical Inquiries into Law* 9 (2008): 239–70.

Arneson, Richard. "Distributive Ethics and Basic Capability Equality: 'Good Enough' Is not Enough," in *Capabilities Equality: Basic Issues and Problems*. Edited by Alexander Kaufman, pp. 17–43. New York: Routledge, 2006.

"Egalitarianism and the Undeserving Poor," *Journal of Political Philosophy* 5 (1997): 327–50.

"Equality and Equal Opportunity for Welfare," *Philosophical Studies* 56 (1989): 77–93.

"Luck Egalitarianism and Prioritarianism," *Ethics*, 110 (2000): 339–49.

"Luck Egalitarianism: An Interpretation and Defense," *Philosophical Topics* 32 (2004): 1–20.

"What, if Anything, Renders All Humans Morally Equal?," in *Singer and His Critics*. Edited by Dale Jamieson, pp. 103–28. Oxford: Blackwell, 1999.

Banfield, Edward. *The Unheavenly City*. Boston: Little, Brown and Company, 1968.

Barry, Nicholas. "Defending Luck Egalitarianism," *Journal of Applied Philosophy* 23 (2006): 89–107.

Bratman, Michael. *Intention, Plans, and Practical Reason*. Cambridge, MA: Harvard University Press, 1987.

Brighouse, Harry, and Swift, Adam. "Equality, Priority, and Positional Goods," *Ethics* 116 (2006): 471–97.

Carens, Joseph. *Equality, Moral Incentives, and the Market: An Essay in Utopian Politico-Economic Theory*. University of Chicago Press, 1981.

Carter, Ian. "Basic Equality and the Site of Egalitarian Justice," *Economics and Philosophy* 29 (2013): 21–41.

"Respect and the Basis of Equality," *Ethics* 121 (2011): 538–71.

Casal, Paula. "Why Sufficiency Is Not Enough," *Ethics* 117 (2007): 296–326.

Chalmers, David. *The Conscious Mind: In Search of a Fundamental Theory.* Oxford University Press, 1996.

Cohen, Gerald. "Luck and Equality: A Reply to Hurley," *Philosophy and Phenomenological Research* 72 (2006): 439–46.

"On the Currency of Egalitarian Justice," *Ethics* 99 (1989): 906–47.

Rescuing Justice and Equality. Cambridge, MA: Harvard University Press, 2008.

Dworkin, Ronald. "Equality, Luck and Hierarchy," *Philosophy and Public Affairs* 31 (2003): 190–98.

"In Defense of Equality," *Social Philosophy and Policy* 1 (1983): 24–40.

Justice for Hedgehogs. Cambridge, MA: Harvard University Press, 2011.

A Matter of Principle. Cambridge, MA: Harvard University Press, 1985.

Sovereign Virtue. Cambridge, MA: Harvard University Press, 2000.

"Sovereign Virtue Revisited," *Ethics* 113 (2002): 106–43.

Taking Rights Seriously. Cambridge, MA: Harvard University Press, 1977.

"What Is Equality? Part 1: Equality of Welfare," *Philosophy and Public Affairs* 10 (1981): 185–246.

"What Is Equality? Part 2: Equality of Resources," *Philosophy and Public Affairs* 10 (1981): 283–345.

Feinberg, Joel. *Doing and Deserving.* Princeton University Press, 1979.

Fleurbaey, Marc. "Egalitarian Opportunities," *Law and Philosophy* 20 (2001): 499–530.

"Equal Opportunity or Equal Social Outcome?," *Economics and Philosophy* 11 (2005): 25–55.

Frankfurt, Harry. "Alternate Possibilities and Moral Responsibility," *Journal of Philosophy* 66 (1969): 829–39.

The Importance of What We Care About. Cambridge University Press, 1988.

Gans, Herbert. *The War against the Poor: The Underclass and Antipoverty Policy.* New York: Basic Books, 1995.

Gutmann, Amy. *Democratic Education.* Princeton University Press, 1987.

Harrington, Michael. *The Other America.* New York: Macmillan, 1962.

Heyd, David, and Miller, G. Franklin. "Life Plans: Do They Give Meaning to Our Lives?," *The Monist* 93 (2010): 17–37.

Holton, Richard. *Willing, Wanting, Waiting.* Oxford University Press, 2009.

Hurley, Susan. *Justice, Luck, and Equality.* Cambridge, MA: Harvard University Press, 2003.

Kagan, Shelly. *The Geometry of Desert.* Oxford University Press, 2012.

Kahneman, Daniel, Slovik, Paul, and Tversky, Amos, eds. *Judgment under Uncertainty: Heuristics and Biases*. Cambridge University Press, 1982.

Kauppinen, Anntui. "Meaningfulness and Time," *Philosophy and Phenomenological Research* 84 (2012): 239–65.

Keller, Simon. "Welfare as Success," *Nous* 43 (2009): 656–83.

Knight, Carl. *Luck Egalitarianism*. University of Edinburgh Press, 2009.

"The Metaphysical Case for Luck Egalitarianism," *Social Theory and Practice* 32 (2006): 173–89.

Korsgaard, Christine. *Creating the Kingdom of Ends*. Cambridge University Press, 1996.

Self-Constitution: Agency, Identity, and Integrity. Oxford University Press, 2009.

The Sources of Normativity. Cambridge University Press, 1996.

Larmore, Charles. *Patterns of Moral Complexity*. Cambridge University Press, 1987.

"The Idea of a Life Plan," *Social Philosophy and Policy* 16 (1999): 96–112.

Lippert-Rasmussen, Kasper. "Egalitarianism, Option Luck, and Responsibility," *Ethics* 111 (2001): 548–79.

"Justice and Bad Luck," *Stanford Encyclopedia of Philosophy* (2009), online, n.p.

Lloyd Thomas, D. A. "Equality within the Limits of Reason Alone," *Mind* 88 (1979): 538–53.

Markovits, Daniel. "Luck Egalitarianism and Political Solidarity," *Theoretical Inquiries into Law* 9 (2008): 271–308.

McKerlie, Dennis. "Equality and Time," *Ethics* 99 (1989): 475–91.

McMahan, Jeff. *The Ethics of Killing: Problems at the Margins of Life*. Oxford University Press, 2002.

Miller, David. *Market, State, and Community: Theoretical Foundations of Market Socialism*. Oxford University Press, 1989.

Nagel, Thomas. *Equality and Partiality*. Oxford University Press, 1991.

The View from Nowhere. Oxford University Press, 1986.

Nozick, Robert. *Anarchy, State, and Utopia*. New York: Basic Books, 1974.

Nussbaum, Martha. *Creating Capabilities: The Human Development Approach*. Cambridge, MA: Harvard University Press, 2011.

Women and Human Development: The Capabilities Approach. Cambridge University Press, 2000.

Olsaretti, Serena, ed. *Justice and Desert*. Oxford University Press, 2003.

Liberty, Desert, and the Market. Cambridge University Press, 2004.

Otsuka, Michael. "Luck, Insurance, and Equality," *Ethics* 113 (2002): 40–54.

Parfit, Derek. "Equality or Priority?," in *The Idea of Equality*. Edited by Matthew Clayton and Andrew Williams, pp. 81–125. Basingstoke: Palgrave Macmillan, 2000.

Pettit, Phillip. "Freedom and Probability: A Comment on Goodin and Jackson," *Philosophy and Public Affairs* 36 (2008): 206–20.

Raibly, Jason R. "Welfare over Time and the Case for Holism," *Philosophical Papers* 41 (2012): 239–65.

Rakowski, Eric. *Equal Justice*. Oxford University Press, 1991.

Rawls, John. *A Theory of Justice*. Cambridge, MA: Harvard University Press, 1971.

"Kantian Constructivism in Moral Theory: The Dewey Lectures 1980," *Journal of Philosophy* 77 (1980): 515–72.

Raz, Joseph. *The Morality of Freedom*. Oxford University Press, 1986.

Riley, Jonathan. "Justice under Capitalism," in *Markets and Justice: Nomos XXXI*. Edited by J. W. Chapman and J. Roland Pennock, pp. 122–62. New York University Press, 1989.

Roemer, John. "A Pragmatic Theory of Responsibility for the Egalitarian Planner," *Philosophy and Public Affairs* 22 (1993): 146–66.

"Equality and Responsibility," *The Boston Review*, 20 (1995): 3–16.

Equality of Opportunity. Cambridge, MA: Harvard University Press, 1998.

Sadurski, Wojchek. *Giving Desert Its Due: Social Justice and Legal Theory*. Dordrecht: Reidel, 1985.

Sandbu, Martin. "On Dworkin's Brute-Luck – Option-Luck Distinction and the Consistency of Brute-Luck Egalitarianism," *Politics, Philosophy, and Economics* 3 (2004): 283–312.

Scheffler, Samuel. *Equality and Tradition*. Oxford University Press, 2010.

"What Is Egalitarianism?," *Philosophy and Public Affairs* 31 (2003): 5–39.

Segall, Shlomi. "In Solidarity with the Imprudent: A Defense of Luck Egalitarianism," *Social Theory and Practice* 33 (2007): 177–98.

Sen, Amartya. *Development as Freedom*. New York: Anchor Books, 1999.

"Equality of What?," in *The Tanner Lectures on Human Values*. Edited by Sterling McMurrin, pp. 195–220. Cambridge University Press, 1980.

Inequality Reexamined. Oxford University Press, 1992.

Sher, George. *Beyond Neutrality: Perfectionism and Politics*. Cambridge University Press, 1997.

Desert. Princeton University Press, 1987.

"Talents and Choices," *Nous* 46 (2012): 375–86.

Who Knew? Responsibility without Awareness. Oxford University Press, 2009.

Singer, Peter. *Animal Liberation*. New York: Avon Books, 1975.

Practical Ethics, Third Edition. Cambridge University Press, 2011.

Smilansky, Saul. "Egalitarian Justice and the Importance of the Free Will Problem," *Philosophia* 25 (1997): 153–61.

Sytsma, Justin, and Machery, Edouard. "The Two Sources of Moral Standing," *Review of Philosophy and Psychology* 3 (2012): 303–24.

Tan, Kok-Chor. "A Defense of Luck Egalitarianism," *Journal of Philosophy* 105 (2008): 665–90.

Temkin, Larry. "Egalitarianism Defended," *Ethics* 110 (2000): 339–49.

Vallentyne, Peter. "Brute Luck and Responsibility," *Philosophy, Politics, and Economics* 7 (2008): 57–80.

"Brute Luck, Option Luck, and Equality of Initial Opportunities," *Ethics* 112 (2002): 529–57.

Velleman, J. David. *Practical Reflection*. Princeton University Press, 1989.

The Possibility of Practical Reason. Oxford University Press, 2000.

Voight, Kristin. "The Harshness Objection: Is Luck Egalitarianism Too Harsh on the Victims of Option Luck?," *Ethical Theory and Moral Practice* 10 (2007): 389–407.

Waldron, Jeremy. "Basic Equality." *New York University Public Law and Legal Theory Working Papers*, 107 (2009): online.

Williams, Bernard. "The Idea of Equality," in *Equality: Selected Readings*. Edited by Louis Pojman and Robert Westmoreland, pp. 91–104. Oxford University Press, 1997.

Moral Luck. Cambridge University Press, 1981.

Wilson, William Julius. *The Truly Disadvantaged*. University of Chicago Press, 1987.

Index